Songs for Renewal

Songs for Renewal

A Devotional Guide to the
Riches of Our Best-Loved
Songs and Hymns

Janet Lindeblad Janzen
with Richard J. Foster

HarperSanFrancisco
An Imprint of HarperCollins*Publishers*

For information about RENOVARÉ write to
RENOVARÉ, 8 Inverness Drive East, Suite 102, Englewood, CO 80112-5609.

Unless otherwise noted, the scripture quotations contained herein are from the New Revised Standard Version of the Bible, copyrighted 1989 by the Division of Christian Education of the National Council of Churches of Christ in the U.S.A., and are used by permission. All rights reserved.

Further credits are listed on page 152 and are considered a continuation of this copyright page.

FIRST HARPERCOLLINS PAPERBACK EDITION PUBLISHED IN 1995

HarperCollins Web Site: http://www.harpercollins.com
HarperCollins®, ▦®, and HarperSanFrancisco™ are trademarks of HarperCollins Publishers Inc.
ISBN 0–06–066742–7 (pbk.)

00 01 02 03 ❖ HAD   11 10 9 8 7 6

To my parents
Rev. H. O. and Roberta Lindeblad

Contents

Acknowledgments

We have been helped in this project by so many people: saints throughout the ages to whose lives we look; authors, hymn writers, and composers of the past from whose work we draw; contemporary colaborers in the faith on whose help we depend. All cannot be named here, but we would like to mention these few.

We are indebted to Greg Shannon and to his grandmother Ruth E. Barber, whose practice of using both Bible and hymnal in her personal meditation sowed a seed that came to fruition in this book. The prayers and encouragement of Carolynn Foster, Paul and Irene Janzen, Miriam Overholt, Cheryl Pohlenz, David Glenn Walker, and our RENOVARÉ groups have been invaluable. Brenda Heard provided efficient, indispensable, and cheerful help with the music typesetting and formatting. Assistance in pulling together resources from a variety of traditions came from Ray and Carolyn Dodson, Blanche Eaton, Warren Farha, Elisabeth Elliot Gren, Barbara Harris, Pat Hommertzheim, John and Donna Mavec, John Leavitt, Mark Lindeblad, Michael Pohlenz, and Don Schroeder. Special thanks are due to Lynda Graybeal of RENOVARÉ and Kandace Hawkinson, Andrea Lewis, and Steve Hanselman of Harper San Francisco.

I would like to thank Richard Foster for his skillful, kind, and encouraging direction; my friend Sue Jung for having the neighborhood kids at her house all summer so that I could write; my parents, Oliver and Roberta Lindeblad, for passing on to me their love for music and the great hymns of the Church along with their Lutheran legacy; my children, Annie and Jacob, for putting up with a preoccupied mom (they gave me an only slightly puzzled look the night I promised them a bedtime story and pulled

The Evangelical Dictionary of Theology from the shelf); my husband, Ken, without whose technical expertise, unfailing patience, and loving support I would not have been able to work on this book; and my Lord Jesus Christ, who has indeed "put a new song in my mouth, a song of praise to our God" (Ps. 40:3). How *amazing* is his grace, and how *great* is his faithfulness!

Janet L. Janzen

The Call of the Heart

In the Christian life devotion and music—praying and singing—are inseparable twins. The apostle Paul urged the early Christian communities both to "pray without ceasing" and to "sing psalms, hymns, and spiritual songs to God" (Col. 3:16). A widely quoted proverb observes that "The one who sings prays twice."

Question: What is it about devotion and music that link them so closely together? Answer: the heart. Prayer is the language of the heart, and music is the medium of the heart.

When praying we are moving beyond merely rational discourse—though we never do violence to our rational faculties. In prayer, somehow (we never fully understand how) our finite human spirit enters into communion with the infinite Spirit of the universe. The very thought of this nearly overcomes us. The circuits of our brain are inadequate to grasp the magnitude of this reality. And, in fact, more is going on in us than brain activity. Spirit touches spirit. What a marvel! What a wonder! To use the imagery of ancient Israel, we are allowed to pass from the Outer Court, through the Inner Court, and into the Holy of Holies and there to burn the eternal flame of prayer on the altar of devotion.

When we enter this prayer-filled life of devotion, however, we often discover that words by themselves are inadequate. When this happens, we are sometimes caught up into wordless wonder, love, and praise. At other times we experience divine communion by means of a heavenly language unknown to our conscious mind. But most frequently we find that the medium of music gives wings to our words and freedom to our devotion.

The psalms are perhaps the richest expression of this medium of devotion. The Psalter is the prayer book of the Church, and, as you may know, it has been set to music from the earliest times. The first Christians continued this tradition of Jewish worship music, often gathering in the catacombs to worship in song. Christians without number have been martyred with songs of devotion on their lips. In the fourth century John Chrysostom used hymns in his battle against the Arian heresy. And in his *Confessions* St. Augustine describes how moved he was by the singing of Ambrose and his congregation.

In the sixth century, under the influence of Gregory the Great, the Gregorian chant along with a more formal liturgy began to dominate the worship experience of the church. This brought many innovations, but it also tended to confine singing to the clergy. However, during the Protestant Reformation, Martin Luther brought worship music back to the people by wedding their own German language to easy-to-sing folk tunes. Out of this grew the great German chorales, still a mainstay of Protestant worship as well as an enduring influence in the world of music, thanks to composers such as J. S. Bach.[1]

The eighteenth-century Wesleyan revival was sung into the hearts of the people through Charles Wesley's sixty-five-hundred-plus hymns, and the nineteenth-century camp meeting revivals gave rise to the gospel hymn. The black spiritual was born to sustain an enslaved people and to give expression to their anguish. Black Gospel music with its jazz influences is one of the few musical forms indigenous to the American scene.[2] In our day the Jesus Movement and its offspring have given us fresh streams of folk and contemporary music, and in France the Taizé Community has led the Church into a prayer-filled worship with a music that is moving in its simplicity. Beyond this are many other streams of music feeding the Church worldwide.

Using as our framework the five great streams that define the balanced vision of Christian life and faith in RENOVARÉ (Contemplative, Holiness, Charismatic, Social Justice, Evangelical), we bring together in this book many of these rich music traditions. We hope you will supplement this modest collection with other devotional and musical resources. If you come from a tradition steeped in gospel songs, you might want to experience some of the powerful German chorales or the worshipful Gregorian chants. If you are more familiar with a liturgical form of worship, you might enjoy some praise choruses or Scripture songs.

In the body of Christ we find tremendous musical diversity, and we are enriched by it all. An intimate refrain like "As the Deer" moves us into a sense of God's immanence, while a traditional hymn such as "Holy God, We Praise Thy Name" reminds us of God's transcendence. "The Trees of the Field" draws us into exuberant worship, while "Jesus, I Am Resting, Resting" calls us to quiet rest. Emotionally and spiritually we need to express a wide range of feelings in our singing and in our devotion. Besides, singing each other's songs is one way we love one another in the Christian fellowship and show forth our unity to the watching world.

The songs in this book of devotion are designed for you to use in your personal meditation, in your families, in your small groups, even in your gathered times of worship. Read them. Pray through them. Memorize them. Meditate over them. Above all, sing them! John Chrysostom reminds us that in singing to God we do not need trained musicians or accompanying instruments; all we need is heartfelt devotion, "For those who sing with the understanding invoke the grace of the Spirit."[3] Jerome notes that even those who are "*kakaphonos*" (bad sounding) can be sweet singers before God if they sing from the heart. And Augustine at times actually preferred listening to a poor-sounding voice over a good one out of a concern that the beautiful music might draw him away from the meaning of the words.[4]

So, do not hesitate to sing out loud! Sing out of obedience. Sing out of love. Sing out of joy. Sing for the glory of God. Sing for the blessing of the saints. Sing for the coming of the kingdom.

Richard J. Foster

Introduction

Hymns embody in a unique way both word and song, theology and art, truth and beauty. They are able to reach and nurture us profoundly. To that end we offer this devotional book. It is meant to help you enter into the riches of our Christian songs and hymns and through them into a closer, more intimate walk with God.

In days past, the Bible and hymnal have been inseparable tools of devotion. Many immigrants coming to the New World brought only two books—Bible and hymnal. Using both they read, sang, and worshiped daily. But in our day the hymnal has fallen out of use in everyday life. It has come to be regarded as part of our church furnishings. Despite the fact that more hymnals are published today than ever before, many Christians do not own one, and we seem to have less singing in our homes. In 1926 hymnologist Louis Benson foresaw an "immediate need to get the church hymnal back into the hands of the people where Luther and Calvin first put it." He observed, "Hymns that are not made personally familiar by devotional reading have not much spiritual influence."[1] We hope that this book will help to get the hymnal out of the pew rack and into the hands, hearts, and lives of the people of God.

This is not a book to read in one sitting. Take time with the devotional readings, allowing perhaps a week for each one. Let each song have ample opportunity to soak in. The readings, questions, and exercises, like the hymns and songs, may be used over and over again. You might try them with your family or in a small group as well as individually. Since this is primarily a devotional book, some of the musical and historical information has been incorporated into the endnotes.

We suggest you memorize the Bible passage that is given as the Scripture Meditation. We have used the New Revised Standard Version unless noted, but feel free to memorize and meditate upon the translation or paraphrase with which you are most comfortable. Do memorize the hymns, perhaps little by little as in time you meditate on them. The rhyme, meter, and music will make them easy to memorize. God's Spirit will draw on this material, and it will return over and over again to strengthen you. And a song can be much more of a heart offering when sung "by heart."

Commonly, the word *hymn* is used to refer to both the words and the music of a song. But technically a hymn is a text and the melody is a *hymn tune*.[2] So when we refer to the writer of a hymn we are referring to the author of the text unless otherwise specified. The writer of the tune is, of course, the composer, and sometimes (more often in contemporary music) the same person writes both. Each hymn tune usually has a name of its own, which appears in this book along with its meter.[3]

We have sought to use inclusive language in our newer hymns, songs, and writings. Older hymns and quotes are, for the most part, in the author's (or translator's) original English words. We follow the example of Jesus, who stressed the Abba character of God, and we have retained the historic, orthodox expression of the Christian faith: God as Father, Son, and Holy Spirit.

In order to suit the needs of individuals and groups and those with various levels of musical training, several formats have been used for the music. We wanted to provide music sufficient to satisfy and yet not so much as would detract from the text. Some of the more common tunes are printed as melody only. Parts for these can be found in many hymnals. (Use the hymnal's "tune index.") Though we have provided some accompaniments, we encourage a cappella singing. This helps us to focus more on the text and the melody rather than on the rendition. Often we think we can't sing a song either alone or in a group without a song leader, pianist, or accompaniment tape.[4] It is almost as if we are afraid of our own voices! But God loves to hear our voices—anytime, anywhere, everywhere. Perhaps that is why he designed our voice as the one musical instrument we always carry with us.

If you are not a trained musician (or maybe especially if you are), do not be overly concerned with a perfect musical performance as you sing these songs. We simply want you to sing them—in any key you find comfortable and any style that seems to fit. In other words, don't be inhibited or limited by the notes on the page. If you don't know the tune, improvise one. Perhaps you know a different *Kyrie, Gloria Patri,* or *Jubilate.* Use it!

Or maybe you know one of these hymns to a different tune. Use it! Try singing these songs in a variety of styles. "Crown Him with Many Crowns," for example, is associated with festive occasions and is often sung, appropriately and inspiringly, in a majestic and stately manner. But you might try it in a mode of quiet worship, perhaps with soft guitar accompaniment, in order to gain a new awareness of the words.

Do not feel obligated to sing all the verses of a given hymn or song.[5] For devotional purposes you may want to sing and focus on just one verse or even one phrase ("Heal Thou gently hearts now broken"[6]). If using stanzas of a hymn selectively, be sure to consider the context as well as the content. Some verses can stand alone; some cannot. For example, if we sing only the first verse of "A Mighty Fortress," we leave the world in the hands of the devil!

We have prayerfully selected songs for this book that we trust will minister to your mind as well as to your spirit. Though this is not a comprehensive collection, we have tried to be representative in our selections not only denominationally but also historically and musically while seeking to embody the essence of the five RENOVARÉ traditions (see appendix A). Singability was an important consideration—a "user-friendly" book for both trained musicians and musicians-in-training (that is, everybody else). Some of the songs included here are RENOVARÉ conference favorites, some are timeless classics, some are popular praise songs, and some were chosen because they aptly reflect one of the RENOVARÉ "streams" of the faith. Some of the more ancient texts are in Latin or Greek. Singing these, using the same words that other believers down through the centuries have used, unites us in a special way with the body of Christ throughout the ages. We hope that this small sampling of songs will spur you on to meditation in your own favorite hymnal, that it will help you find new ways to sing old favorites, and that it will introduce you to songs from other traditions that will become new favorites. *Soli Deo Gloria!*

Songs of Confession

Only to sit and think of God,
Oh what a joy it is!
To think the thought,
To breathe the name,
Earth has no higher bliss.

—*Frederick W. Faber*

These opening songs lay the groundwork for our devotion. They set before us

> *the person of God—"The Apostles' Creed"*
> *the love of God—"Jesus Loves Me"*
> *the grace of God—"Amazing Grace"*
> *the people of God—"The Church's One Foundation"*
> *our response to God—"In the Name of Christ We Gather"*
> *and a doxology of praise to God—"Gloria Patri"*

You see, to think rightly about God is, in an important sense, to have everything right, and to think wrongly about God is to have everything wrong. Our singing and our devotion need to be constantly oriented to and informed by "the knowledge of the glory of God in the face of Christ" (2 Cor. 4:6).

The Apostles' Creed
(Paraphrased)

Author Unknown

AUSTRIAN HYMN (8.7.8.7.D.)
Franz Joseph Haydn, 1797

1. I believe in God the Father, Maker of the heav'n and earth,
2. Suffered under Pontius Pilate, Crucified for me He died;
3. At God's right hand He is seated, till His coming as He said,
4. I believe the Church of Jesus forms one body as a whole.

And in Jesus Christ, our Savior, God's own Son of matchless worth;
Laid within the grave so silent, gates of hell He opened wide.
Final judgment will be meted to the living and the dead,
All are one throughout the ages, with the saints I lift my soul.

Laid aside His heav'nly glory, By the Holy Ghost conceived,
And the stone-sealed tomb was empty, on the third day He arose,
I confess the Holy Spirit has been sent thru Christ the Son,
I believe sins are forgiven, that our bodies will be raised;

Born unto the Virgin Mary, He in whom I have believed.
Into heaven made His entry, Mighty conqueror of His foes.
To apply salvation's merit, God Almighty, Three in One.
Everlasting life in heaven, May God's holy name be praised!

Scripture Reading: 1 Corinthians 15:3–22

This passage contains one of the earliest recorded summaries of the apostles' teaching concerning the Christian faith. In reading it, notice that Paul is merely acting as a messenger. These are things given to him in order that he might pass them on—things of utmost importance. Here are the facts: the death, burial, and resurrection of Christ. Here is the reason: for our sins. Note how Paul devotes the remainder of the passage and of the chapter to the reality of the resurrection.

Scripture Meditation: 1 Corinthians 15:3–5

For I handed on to you as of first importance what I in turn had received: that Christ died for our sins in accordance with the scriptures, and that he was buried, and that he was raised on the third day in accordance with the scriptures.

As you meditate on this Scripture, think of those who have faithfully handed on the gospel to you, not only directly but also down through the ages. Give thanks to God for them. Prayerfully consider the implications in your life of the facts set forth here: Christ died for my sins. His was a real, physical death, evidenced by his burial. Christ was raised from the dead. His was a real, physical resurrection, evidenced by his appearances to the disciples and others. Sing the hymn and notice how these truths are central to it.

Reflecting in Song

This hymn is a paraphrase of the Apostles' Creed, the most widely used statement of belief in all of Christendom. The Apostles' Creed derives from the second-century Old Roman Creed, which was used in a question-and-answer form to instruct and prepare new Christians for baptism. This method of teaching, called "catechesis," provided the main form of religious instruction in the early Church.

Martin Luther believed that the Apostles' Creed along with the Ten Commandments and the Lord's Prayer contained all the essential teaching of the Bible. He confessed, "Although I am a doctor, I have to do just as a child and say word for word every morning and whenever I have time the Lord's Prayer and the Ten Commandments, the Creed and the Psalms."[1]

Singing the Creed has been a common practice in the past, especially in the liturgical churches. Sing the first three verses of the Creed and note its Trinitarian nature. Affirm your faith in the Father, the Son, and the Holy Spirit. Now sing the fourth verse, noting its emphasis on the Church universal. Think of Christians throughout the ages—past, present, and future—singing and saying these same words. Rejoice that you are among them!

Questions of Examen and Exercises of Devotion

1. Are there parts of the Apostles' Creed I have difficulty affirming? Are there beliefs I need to examine in light of the Creed?
2. Why has this particular statement of Christian faith endured? What aspects of it do I personally find helpful and sustaining?
3. For one week post this paraphrase of the Creed on the refrigerator or in your car and sing it as often as possible.
4. Write down three ways the affirmations of the Creed can help to improve your relationships with your children or spouse or close friends.

The Prayer of the Heart

Lord God almighty, thank you that this faith once delivered to the saints is not just nebulous speculations pulled out of thin air, but rather bedrock beliefs grounded in specific historical realities. May my life increasingly conform to these truths and ever bring glory to you, O God, Father, Son, and Holy Spirit. Amen.

Jesus Loves Me

JESUS LOVES ME (7.7.7.7. with refrain)

Anna B. Warner, 1860

William Bradbury, 1862

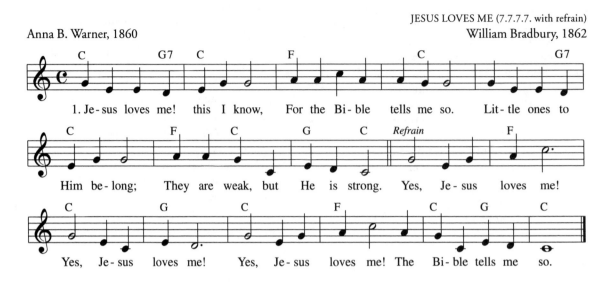

1. Je-sus loves me! this I know, For the Bi-ble tells me so. Lit-tle ones to Him be-long; They are weak, but He is strong.

Refrain

Yes, Je-sus loves me! Yes, Je-sus loves me! Yes, Je-sus loves me! The Bi-ble tells me so.

2. Jesus from His throne on high,
   Came into this world to die;
   That I might from sin be free,
   Bled and died upon the tree.

3. Jesus loves me!—He who died
   Heaven's gate to open wide!
   He will wash away my sin,
   Let His little child come in.

4. Jesus, take this heart of mine;
   Make it pure and wholly Thine:
   Thou hast bled and died for me,
   I will henceforth live for Thee.

Scripture Reading: John 15:9–17

As you read this passage, note that several interdependent love relationships are described here: the Father's love for the Son, the Son's love for his disciples, the disciples' love for one another. See how this love is acted out in obedience and sacrifice. Jesus does not just tell his disciples about love; he demonstrates it to them.

Scripture Meditation: John 15:9

> *As the Father has loved me, so I have loved you;*
> *abide in my love.*

Take some time to reflect on these words of Jesus. Do not be in a hurry. When you are ready, sing softly the first verse of "Jesus Loves Me." Gently repeat the affirmation, "Yes, Jesus loves me," and meditate upon the words. Gradually intersperse them with breath prayers such as, "Help me feel loved," "Thank you for your love," "I love you, Lord Jesus." Continue to pray that the love of Jesus may be a living, heartfelt reality in your life.

Reflecting in Song

This is one of the most-loved Christian songs of the past century. It has been translated into many languages and is sung all over the world. It has enjoyed special popularity in China and throughout the Pacific Rim, perhaps due to the simple pentatonic (five-tone) scale used in its melody, which gives it an Eastern flavor. Also, the words convey the profoundest possible truth in the greatest possible simplicity.

These verses were first published in 1860 in a novel written by Anna B. Warner.[2] In the story a friend sings this song to comfort a young boy who is dying. William Bradbury later wrote a tune for the verses and added the refrain. Others have added verses or changed words, resulting in several different versions of the song.[3]

Read through the verses, seeking to enter into their meaning. See how deeply theological, yet how simple it all is. Everything basic to Christian theology is here— revelation, incarnation, redemption, salvation, sanctification. In verse four we make a personal dedication of ourselves in response to all that God has done for us. It is no wonder that Karl Barth, when asked to sum up the essence of his theological position, responded with, "Jesus loves me! This I know, for the Bible tells me so."

Now sing the song and think of your earliest memories of it. "Jesus Loves Me" is often the first song learned in childhood, and, as in the novel, it has accompanied many in their entry into eternity. A dear friend, Chuck, after suffering from cancer for many years, recently took that journey we will all one day take. Late one night, after enduring several especially painful months, he knew that God's time had come. Quietly and tenderly Chuck began singing "Jesus Loves Me" and praying for God to receive his spirit. In the early hours of the morning he was indeed welcomed into the arms of Jesus.

We are never too old, never too sophisticated, never too theologically astute to return to this simple truth. Jesus himself reminds us, "Whoever does not receive the kingdom of God as a little child will never enter it" (Mark 10:15).

And so as you sing this song once again, receive the love of Jesus into your mind and heart. Give thanks. Sing quietly the last verse again, using these words as a refrain: "I love you, Jesus . . . Because you love me so."

Questions of Examen and Exercises of Devotion

1. Have I at certain times in the past felt the love of Jesus to be especially real?
2. What things might hinder a fuller realization of his love now?
3. Next time you face a situation in which you feel unloved or unlovely, quietly sing the refrain of this song.
4. Think of someone you know who is particularly in need of the love of Jesus. Do something specific to bring his love to him or her.

The Prayer of the Heart

Thank you, Jesus, that I can never outgrow your love. Regardless of how many places I may go or the number of accomplishments I may make, I am always sustained by your love. Thank you, Lord. Help me to drink often at the wellspring of your love. Amen.

Amazing Grace

John Newton, 1779 (st. 4, anon.)

NEW BRITAIN (C.M.)
From *Virginia Harmony,* 1831

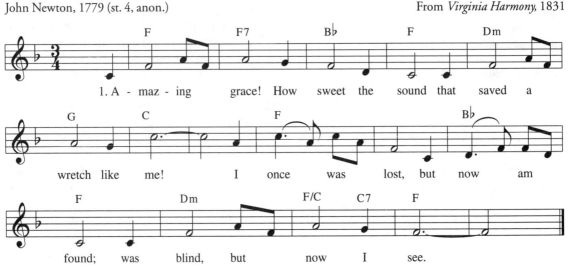

1. A - maz - ing grace! How sweet the sound that saved a wretch like me! I once was lost, but now am found; was blind, but now I see.

2. 'Twas grace that taught my heart to fear,
   And grace my fears relieved;
   How precious did that grace appear
   The hour I first believed.

3. Through many dangers, toils, and snares,
   I have already come;
   'Tis grace that brought me safe thus far,
   And grace will lead me home.

4. When we've been there ten thousand years,
   Bright shining as the sun,
   We've no less days to sing God's praise
   Than when we'd first begun.

Scripture Reading: Romans 5

The essence of the gospel is set forth in this passage, namely, that we have peace with God through our Lord Jesus Christ. Romans 5 is like an explanation and exposition of John 3:16. Keep that verse in mind ("For God so loved the world . . .") as you read this passage. See how Paul's words relate to those of Jesus. Note how many times Paul uses the word *grace*. Now, sing the hymn.

Scripture Meditation: Romans 5:8

But God proves his love for us in that while we still were sinners Christ died for us.

Read through this verse slowly several times. Insert your name in place of *us* and repeat the passage. Now, use the word *me* and repeat it again. Notice that the word *proves* is in the present tense. Yes, Christ died once for all, but God continually proves his love to us, over and over again. Redemption and salvation are both present-tense realities. Ponder the meaning of *while we still were sinners*. It is difficult to forgive those who don't know they've hurt or wronged us. It is harder still if they know but refuse to acknowledge their offense. And it is nearly impossible if they persistently repeat the transgression. To give up one of our children for such a person would be humanly unthinkable. Yet God gave his only Son for just such sinners—you and me.

Reflecting in Song

Few things amaze us these days. The nightly news provides us with live footage of the spectacular, and the hi-tech entertainment industry takes us regularly to regions beyond human imagining. Many of us, having heard and sung about grace since childhood, are jaded by it rather than amazed by it.

But John Newton (eighteenth century) never ceased to be amazed at God's grace. His devout mother, who had taught him the Scriptures and prayed that he would become a minister, died when he was seven. Taken to sea with his father, young John soon abandoned the faith of his childhood. Before the age of twenty he was put on a slave-trading ship and began a life of "continued godlessness and profanity."[4] When twenty-three, however, John happened to read Thomas à Kempis's *Imitation of Christ*. Soon afterward, while facing shipwreck during a fierce storm at sea, he placed his faith in the God he had been ridiculing. Now, imagine yourself in Newton's place as you sing the first verse of his hymn.

God heard and answered the heartfelt prayers of John's mother. This is God's prevenient grace at work—the "grace that taught my heart to fear." Prevenient grace is the "hound of heaven" grace that goes before and prepares the way for saving grace—the grace that relieves our fears and brings peace with God. As you sing verse two, notice how Newton reflects on both kinds of grace.

The work of grace dramatically transformed John Newton. He gave up his slave trading and became a minister of the gospel. His influence was substantial, and his preaching inspired William Wilberforce, a Member of Parliament, to lead the fight for the abolition of slavery in England. At age eighty, with failing eyesight and ill health, Newton was advised to stop preaching. His response: "What! Shall the old African blasphemer stop while he can speak?"[5] As with John Newton, God's sanctifying and perfecting grace continues its work throughout our lives in order that he who began a good work in us may "bring it to completion at the day of Jesus Christ" (Phil. 1:6, RSV). Make this your meditation as you sing the last two verses.

Questions of Examen and Exercises of Devotion

1. What circumstances in my life are examples of God's prevenient grace?
2. When did I first become aware of God's saving grace?
3. Consider ways in which God's sanctifying and perfecting grace is at work in you now, and how you might allow it to work further.
4. In view of the grace given to you, practice giving grace to others; for example, forgive an unacknowledged offense.

The Prayer of the Heart

O Lord, I receive your grace and acceptance of me. Thank you for your prevailing grace. It is indeed amazing! Amen.

The Church's One Foundation

AURELIA (7.6.7.6.D.)

Samuel J. Stone, 1866

Samuel S. Wesley, 1864

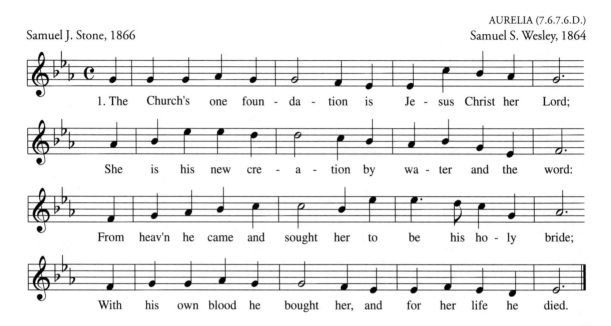

1. The Church's one foun - da - tion is Je - sus Christ her Lord;
She is his new cre - a - tion by wa - ter and the word:
From heav'n he came and sought her to be his ho - ly bride;
With his own blood he bought her, and for her life he died.

2. Elect from every nation, yet one o'er all the earth,
Her charter of salvation: one Lord, one faith, one birth;
One holy name she blesses, partakes one holy food,
And to one hope she presses with every grace endued.

3. Though with a scornful wonder we see her sore oppressed,
By schisms rent asunder, by heresies distressed:
Yet saints their watch are keeping, their cry goes up, "How long?"
And soon the night of weeping shall be the morn of song.

4. 'Mid toil and tribulation, and tumult of her war,
She waits the consummation of peace forevermore,
Till with the vision glorious her longing eyes are blest,
And the great Church victorious shall be the Church at rest.

5. Yet she on earth hath union with God, the Three in One,
And mystic sweet communion with those whose rest is won:
O happy ones and holy! Lord, give us grace that we,
Like them, the meek and lowly, on high may dwell with thee.

Scripture Reading: Ephesians 2:11–22
The unity of the Church of Jesus Christ is the focus of this passage as it is of much of Ephesians. Consider the long-standing enmity and prejudice that existed between Jews and Gentiles in the first century. They had diverse ethnic and cultural backgrounds and different

religious practices. Yet Christ broke down the barriers, bringing peace with one another and with God. Christ is not only the foundation; he is also the mortar that holds the Church together.

Scripture Meditation: Ephesians 2:19–20

So then you are no longer strangers and aliens, but you are citizens with the saints and also members of the household of God, built upon the foundation of the apostles and prophets, with Christ Jesus himself as the cornerstone.

In your meditation reflect on a time when you felt like a stranger or foreigner. How wonderful to meet a friend or to come back home after such a time! In the Church of Jesus Christ there are no strangers; we are always at home. Perhaps you would now like to give thanks that you are a part of God's household. Then, too, invite God to break down any barriers that separate you from other members of his family or keep you from feeling at home with him.

Reflecting in Song

This hymn was written by Samuel John Stone as part of a series of twelve hymns based on the Apostles' Creed. These verses focus on the article, "The Holy Catholic Church, the Communion of Saints." Read through the hymn and notice the central theme in each verse:

1. Christ, the Center
2. The people of God
3. Contending for the faith
4. The longing for consummation
5. Glorification

Which of these themes do you most identify with at this point in your life?

As you sing through each verse of this hymn, try to imagine Christians from other centuries and different cultures. What struggles did they face? What ambiguities did they have to deal with? How did their faithfulness or disobedience affect others—indeed, the very course of human history?

Now, focus your attention on the second verse. Such diversity in the body of Christ—every tongue, every nation, every people. Such unity in the body of Christ—one Lord, one faith, one birth. Consider ways

you can celebrate the cultural and ethnic diversity *and* the essential and central unity we have in Christ.

The third and fourth verses of this song concentrate on the warfare and tribulation the Church must face—enemies from within and without. Consider your own struggle, personally and corporately, in the community of faith. Perhaps you have endured some painful battles; even so, be encouraged by the words of the writer to the Hebrews: "You have not yet resisted to the point of blood" (Heb. 12:4, KJV). Remember, the day is coming when "the great Church victorious shall be the Church at rest."

Finally, soak in that last verse with its wonderful descriptions of union and communion. Did you catch how Samuel Stone brings together the oneness we have with God with the oneness we will have with the Church universal? We have yet to experience the full reality of that oneness. Often it is said jokingly (but truly):

To live above with saints we love;
O that will be glory.
To live below with saints we know;
Well, that's a different story.

Regardless of our imperfect efforts, let's rejoice in the unity of heart and mind God *does* give us in our work together.

Questions of Examen and Exercises of Devotion

1. How deep is my commitment to the community of faith, the Church?
2. How foundational is Christ to the life of my family? Of my church?
3. Do one thing this month that will promote a deeper oneness in the body of Christ.
4. Read a well-written biography of a Christian from an earlier century or from another culture as a way of participating more fully in "the communion of the saints."

The Prayer of the Heart

Thank you, Lord, for those who have been valiant for the Truth in past generations. Thank you for those I know by name. Thank you, too, for all those nameless and faceless millions upon millions who have walked cheerfully over the earth in the power of God. May I do the same. Amen.

In the Name of Christ We Gather

(A Hymn for RENOVARÉ)

HYFRYDOL (8.7.8.7.D.)

Janet L. Janzen, 1989

Rowland H. Prichard, 1830

1. In the name of Christ we gather, out of love we seek His will.
2. Let us live a life of prayer and ho-li-ness be-fore the Lord;
3. Though the path a-head be nar-row, Je-sus makes our bur-den light;

As dis-ci-ples, through His grace may we our cov-e-nant ful-fill.
Walk, re-joic-ing in the Spi-rit and o-be-dience to God's Word,
Gives us joy and peace in tri-al, fi-nal vic-t'ry in the fight.

Now, en-cour-ag-ing one a-no-ther, on His Spi-rit we de-pend:
Serv-ing oth-ers with com-pas-sion, to the world this mes-sage send:
Giv-ing glo-ry un-to God, may we be faith-ful to the end:

Je-sus Christ, our ev-er-liv-ing Sav-ior, Teach-er, Lord, and Friend.
Je-sus Christ is ev-er-liv-ing Sav-ior, Teach-er, Lord, and Friend!
Je-sus Christ, our ev-er-liv-ing Sav-ior, Teach-er, Lord, and Friend.

Scripture Reading: Hebrews 10:19–25

Read the passage slowly, noting the access we have to God because of the blood of Jesus. This allows us to come with true hearts and a full assurance of faith. Note the purification given us by the blood of Christ and the command to hold fast to the confession of our hope. Finally, see the privilege and responsibility we have to provide one another with loving, nurturing accountability.

Scripture Meditation: Hebrews 10:23–24

Begin your meditation by singing the hymn. Become aware of the range of aspirations and hopes expressed in it. See how it centers on Christ. Especially note the refrain, "Jesus Christ, our everliving Savior, Teacher, Lord, and Friend."

When you are ready, turn your attention to the text for meditation.

> *Let us hold fast the confession of our hope without wavering, for he who promised is faithful; and let us consider how to stir up one another to love and good works (RSV).*

Speak it out loud. Read it silently. Meditate on the meaning of "the confession of our hope." Give thanks for the faithfulness of God. Consider those under your care and the ways you might be able to encourage them toward "love and good works."

Reflecting in Song

This song takes to heart the words of St. Basil that the Holy Spirit blends "the delight of melody with doctrines in order that through the pleasantness and softness of the sound we might receive unawares what was useful in the words."[6] It sets forth some of the basic convictions of RENOVARÉ—the centrality of Christ, our commitment to one another as a community of faith, the importance of the five great streams of life and faith, and more.

Sing the first verse. These words grow out of our weekly experience in the Spiritual Formation Groups. These meetings involve a covenant to live as disciples of Jesus and a commitment to help one another live out the life of that covenant (see appendix A). Sing these words as your personal confession to live as a disciple—an apprentice, if you will—of Jesus. Speak a prayer of receiving Christ as your life.

When you are ready, sing the second verse. Notice how each of the five dimensions of the spiritual life is held up to view: the Contemplative Tradition—the prayer-filled life; the Holiness Tradition—the virtuous life; the Charismatic Tradition—the Spirit-empowered life; the Social Justice Tradition—the compassionate life; and the Evangelical Tradition—the Word-centered life. Consider how these traditions have nurtured your spiritual life. Give thanks to God for these good influences. Do you see traditions that you would like to learn more about? Ask God for help and guidance to move you into these newer realms.

Now, sing the hymn one last time, centering on "Jesus Christ our everliving Savior, Teacher, Lord, and Friend." Jesus Christ is alive and here to teach us himself. He has not contracted laryngitis. His voice is not hard to hear. His vocabulary is not difficult to understand. And he is among us in all his offices: he is our Savior to forgive us, our Teacher to instruct us, our Lord to rule us, and our Friend to come alongside us. How do you need Jesus to function in your life today? Invite his life to come upon you. Allow his love to conquer you. Receive his grace to enable you.

Questions of Examen and Exercises of Devotion

1. How have I experienced Christ most fully: as Savior, Teacher, Lord, or Friend?
2. Of the five dimensions of the Christian life mentioned in verse two, in which am I strongest? Where do I need to grow?
3. Plan some definite steps you can undertake in the next few months to immerse yourself more fully in one of the five traditions—Contemplative, Holiness, Charismatic, Social Justice, Evangelical.
4. Pray the third verse of the song for yourself or for a loved one ("Though the path ahead be narrow, Jesus, make my/her/his burden light. . . . Be my/her/his everliving Savior, Teacher, Lord, and Friend.")

The Prayer of the Heart

Dear Jesus, thank you for being my everliving Savior, Teacher, Lord, and Friend. Help me to grow as your disciple, and help me to encourage others in their walk with you. Amen.

Gloria Patri
(Glory Be to the Father)

CASWALL (6.5.6.5.)

Paraphrased by Janet L. Janzen

Friedrich Filitz, 1847

1. Glo - ry to the Fa - ther, Glo - ry to the Son,
2. God of end - less a - ges, Ev - er - more shall be

Glo - ry to the Spi - rit, Bles - sed Three in One.
As in the be - gin - ning, Through e - ter - ni - ty.

Words © Janet Lindeblad Janzen, 1994

Scripture Reading:
Psalm 41:13, 72:18–19, 89:52, 106:48, 150

The book of Psalms is divided into five smaller books, each of which ends with a doxology or statement of praise. Read these five doxologies and notice the similarities. Be aware of the divisions that they mark. Observe that the book as a whole ends with several entire psalms of praise, making a grand, concluding doxology.

Scripture Meditation: Psalm 72:18–19

Blessed be the LORD, the God of Israel,
who alone does wondrous things.
Blessed be his glorious name forever;
may his glory fill the whole earth. Amen and Amen.

Repeat this Scripture until it is familiar. Pause, and give time to God in praise and adoration. Put away stray thoughts. Let go of the clock and the pressures of the day. Speak aloud your praise to God. Sing praises to him as the Spirit brings songs to mind.

Reflecting in Song

The word *doxology* comes from two Greek words: *doxa,* meaning "glory," and *logos,* meaning "word." In doxology we speak forth words of glory and praise to God. The use of doxologies in worship dates back to the days of the synagogue, as evidenced by their placement in the book of Psalms. In his *Rule* of 525, St. Benedict made it official practice in Christian worship to close each psalm with a doxology. The *Gloria Patri,* one of the ancient doxologies of the Church, was frequently used in that context.

The *Gloria Patri* is traditionally known as the Lesser Doxology, the Greater Doxology being the *Gloria in Excelsis*—a hymn based upon the song sung by the angels at the birth of Christ. Both date back to the second century. The song commonly called "The Doxology" ("Praise God from whom all blessings flow") is probably the best known of all doxologies. It is of much later origin, written by Thomas Ken in 1692.

Christians of many denominations, both liturgical and nonliturgical, include the *Gloria Patri* in their worship. It is sung to many different tunes and is sometimes paraphrased. The words may be familiar:

> Glory be to the Father, and to the Son, and to the Holy Ghost; as it was in the beginning, is now, and ever shall be, world without end. Amen.

Sing the song as offered here. This paraphrase is set to a nineteenth-century German melody.

A Trinitarian doxology, the *Gloria Patri* is drawn from Jesus' words: ". . . baptizing them in the name of the Father, and of the Son, and of the Holy Ghost" (Matt. 28:19, KJV). The doctrine of the Trinity has been a touchstone of orthodox Christianity since the fourth century, when it was formalized by various councils and affirmed in the Nicene Creed. Though the word *Trinity* does not occur in Scripture, the doctrine is inherent in it: within the one divine nature of God are three "persons" all coequal and coeternally God. The Old Testament especially emphasizes the unity and uniqueness of God: "The LORD our God is *one* LORD" (Deut. 6:4). Yet the New Testament also refers to God as Father, God as Son, and God as Spirit.

We cannot entirely understand the concept—one essence, three persons. It has been the subject of study, speculation, and controversy. Analogies and explanations abound, but they invariably come up short. When we as finite human beings try to explain the infinite, we eventually run out of words. Admitting this is not an intellectual cop-out, but a humble acceptance of our limitations. God created our minds, and he wants us to use them. We may inquire to the furthest limits of our intellect, and even there we will find him as we explore new realms of his truth, his beauty, his goodness. But though we know God truly and increasingly, we will never know him exhaustively. Always there will be unfathomable mysteries that we will never completely comprehend. But we can break forth into doxology: "O the depth of the riches and wisdom and knowledge of God! How unsearchable are his judgments and how inscrutable his ways! . . . To him be the glory forever. Amen" (Rom. 11:33, 36). Sing the *Gloria Patri.* Worship this infinite, triune God who loves you personally with an inexhaustible, unending love.

Questions of Examen and Exercises of Devotion

1. With which person of the Trinity do I most frequently relate?
2. What act could I do today that would honor God?
3. Many hymns and songs include a form of the *Gloria Patri,* for example, "Now Thank We All Our God" (last verse), "Glorify Thy Name" by Donna Adkins ("Father, Jesus, Spirit . . . Glorify Thy Name"). Notice these and use them in worship.
4. Make up your own *Gloria Patri* or song of praise to the Trinity.

The Prayer of the Heart

Glory be to you, mighty God, Lord of all! I praise you, heavenly Father. I worship you, Jesus Christ. I bless you, Holy Spirit. May your name be glorified in all the earth, and in heaven above, throughout all eternity. Amen.

Songs of Contemplation

One may also sing without voice, the mind resounding inwardly.
For we sing, not to men, but to God, who can hear our hearts and
enter into the silences of our minds.

—*John Chrysostom*

God speaks without ceasing to his children, but the outward clatter of our world and the inward distraction of our hearts often deafen us. In contemplation we are learning

> *to turn away from the din without,*
> *to speak peace to the storm within, and*
> *to listen, silent and still, to the voice of the true Shepherd.*

To do this involves "the deep hush of the whole soul," as François Fénelon reminds us. He adds, "We must bend the ear, because it is a gentle and delicate voice, only heard by those who no longer hear anything else."

Music, rightly used, does not break this silence of the soul but continues it. When we sing, "Jesus, I am resting, resting in the joy of what thou art," we sing with a heart that is listening, resting, entering into the greatness of God's loving heart.

As the Deer

Martin Nystrom

Martin Nystrom

1. As the deer pant-eth for the wa-ter so my soul long-eth af-ter Thee.

You a-lone are my heart's de-sire, and I long to wor-ship Thee.

Refrain
You a-lone are my strength, my shield, To You a-lone may my spir-it yield.

You a-lone are my heart's de-sire, and I long to wor-ship Thee.

2. You're my friend and You are my brother
   Even though You are a King.
   I love You more than any other,
   So much more than anything.

3. I want You more than gold or silver,
   Only You can satisfy.
   You alone are the real joy giver
   And the apple of my eye.

Scripture Reading: Psalm 42:1–11

As you read this psalm, note the longing of the writer for God. See the tears, the discouragement, the hoping. Be especially attentive to the refrain in verses five and eleven. Note how the psalmist speaks to his own soul, urging it not to be cast down but to hope in God.

Scripture Meditation: Psalm 42:1–2

Begin your meditation by singing this song. As you sing gently, allow your own heart longing for God to rise up and all competing desires to fade into the background. Be sensitive to any movements of the Spirit within of faith, hope, and love. As you are ready, move your attention gently to Psalm 42:1–2. Intersperse your meditation upon the text of Scripture with heart prayers of longing and thirsting.

> As the deer longs for flowing streams,
>   so my soul longs for you, O God.
> My soul thirsts for God,
>   for the living God.

Reflecting in Song

When you are ready, meditate more deeply on the song itself. Note the all-encompassing yearning for God expressed in the words. Sing verse one again, focusing this time on the image of thirst. Jesus says, "Let anyone who is thirsty come to me, and let the one who believes in me drink" (John 7:37–38). Drink of Jesus now, allowing his life to well up within you like rivers of living water. Invite his life to come forth like "a spring of water gushing up to eternal life" (John 4:14). Wait quietly, receiving anything the Spirit wants to impart to you.

Sing the refrain, this time centering on the ways God is your strength and your shield. Prayerfully speak the confession of Psalm 27:5, "[God] will hide me in his shelter in the day of trouble; he will conceal me under the cover of his tent; he will set me high on a rock." Allow God's strength and protection to surround you and cover you and shield you. Pray for this in the specifics of your relationships and the activities of your days. Receive his protection, his love, his care.

Sing the entire song again, giving special attention to the second verse, which invites us to experience God as our friend. Even though God is the sovereign of the universe, he is welcoming us into his friendship. "I do not call you servants any longer," says Jesus, "but I have called you friends" (John 15:15). Receive the friendship of God. Receive the companionship of God. Receive the embrace of God. Do not be afraid; it is the King who is inviting you to himself.

Questions of Examen and Exercises of Devotion

1. What are the two or three things in my life that could potentially rival God as "the apple of my eye"?
2. What could I do this next week that would deepen my longing for God?
3. Ask God to show you if there are things in your past that hinder you from embracing his friendship.
4. Commit the refrain to memory. Enjoy brief times of worship throughout the day as you sing or speak it.

The Prayer of the Heart

Loving God, place in my heart a deep unquenchable thirst for you. Like the deer let me drink and be satisfied, but also like the deer give me the craving to always come back for more. Thank you, Lord. Thank you. Amen.

More Precious than Silver

Lynn De Shazo

Lynn De Shazo

Lord, You are more pre-cious than sil-ver,

Lord, You are more cost-ly than gold;

Lord, you are more beau-ti-ful than dia-monds, and

noth-ing I de-sire com-pares with You.

Scripture Reading: Luke 7:36–50

Picture yourself as a guest at Simon's dinner party. See the unself-conscious abandon with which this woman, an unnamed but notorious sinner, flings herself at Jesus' feet and proceeds to wash, kiss, and anoint them. Observe the host's unspoken but apparent disdain. Are there parts of you that concur with his assessment? Notice that Jesus perceives Simon's thoughts and responds to them. But, rather than condemning this woman with the sordid past, Jesus extols her act of devotion and love.

Scripture Meditation: Luke 7:47

Her sins, which were many, have been forgiven; hence she has shown great love. But the one to whom little is forgiven, loves little.

Put yourself in the place of the woman in this story, and sing this song. Meditating upon this Scripture verse, consider all that Jesus has forgiven you. Sing the song again as your own love song to him, your own act of devotion.

Reflecting in Song

Love for Jesus is lavish, demonstrative, unashamed love. Jesus welcomes and blesses those who show him this kind of love. The Evangelical Sisters of Mary, like the woman in the Scripture, delight in showing love to Jesus. This primarily Lutheran sisterhood was founded in postwar Germany when several young women felt the need to repent on behalf of their nation. As they entered into the grief and pain of the Father's heart, God drew them together in a special way. They covenanted to live as a community, depending only upon God and desiring to bring only joy to his heart. They constructed their first building with their own hands out of bricks gathered from the bombed-out ruins of Darmstadt, Germany. There are now branches of this community on every continent, proclaiming love to Jesus and showing forth his love to the world.

Recognizing that Jesus is even today the object of much public scorn and hatred, the sisters give open testimony of love for him—not in pretentious displays of piety but in genuine demonstrations of devotion, such as humble worship services in the midst of busy shopping malls. They also show love to Jesus in deeply personal ways, living lives of daily repentance and leading others into a closer walk with Christ.

In her little book, *My All for Him,* Mother Basilea Schlink,[1] a founder of the sisterhood, writes of the importance of having Jesus as our first love and of expressing our love to him. She reminds us, "Jesus is yearning to have fellowship with us and to hear words of love drop from our lips. He is waiting for us. . . . He wants to speak to us in our hearts, to cultivate love's intimate relationship with us."

But perhaps a question has arisen in your mind: "How can I honestly experience and express this 'first love' for Jesus? Is it something I can will to do, or is it an emotional state into which I must work myself? What is the key?" The answer is the same as it was for the woman in the story and the same it was for the Sisters of Mary: the key is repentance. It is recognizing just how very much we have been forgiven. She who is forgiven much, loves much.

Once again, sing this simple song of adoration to him who has redeemed you not with silver and gold but with his holy and precious blood. Sing, and let Jesus hear words of love from your lips. Sing, and confess with the psalmist, "There is nothing on earth that I desire other than you" (Psalm 73:25).

Questions of Examen and Exercises of Devotion

1. What things rival Jesus as the "first love" of my life?
2. In what tangible way might I show love to Jesus during the coming week?
3. When you next witness an instance of mocking or scorn for Jesus or the ridiculing of his name, make it a special point to speak words of love to him in your heart.
4. In the next week or so, do a literal act of service to one of the "little ones" in your world as a love action to Jesus.

The Prayer of the Heart

Lord, how very precious you are. Help me to see my sin in the light of your love. I love you, Jesus. Help me to express my love even before I feel it. And may I not be ashamed of my love for you. Amen.

Be Thou My Vision

Trad. Irish, c. 8th century
Tr. Mary E. Byrne, 1905
Versified by Eleanor H. Hull, 1912
Vs. 3, Janet L. Janzen, 1991

SLANE (10.10.10.10)
Traditional Irish Melody

1. Be thou my Vi-sion, O Lord of my heart; Naught be all else to me, save that thou art; Thou my best thought, by day or by night, Wak-ing or sleep-ing, thy pres-ence my light.

2. Be thou my Wisdom, and thou my true Word,
I ever with thee and thou with me, Lord;
Thou and thou only, first in my heart,
High King of heaven, my Treasure thou art.

3. Be thou my Bridegroom, my Love to the end,
Thou my Companion and thou my dear Friend;
Thou my Desire, for thee do I long,
Thou my Fulfillment, my Joy and my Song.

4. Be thou my Breastplate, my Sword for the fight;
Thou my whole Armour, and thou my true Might;
Thou my soul's Shelter, thou my strong Tower;
Raise thou me heavenward, great Power of my power.

5. High King of heaven, my victory won,
May I reach heaven's joys, O bright heaven's Son!
Heart of my own heart, whatever befall,
Still be my Vision, O Ruler of all.

Scripture Reading: Matthew 17:1–9

In this account of the transfiguration, we join some of the disciples in catching a first glimpse of the magnificent glory of Christ. Observe how Jesus refers to it as a "vision" (v. 9). This in no way implies unreality. A vision, as given by God, allows us to see things with a finer sight. On this occasion Jesus' true identity as the exalted Messiah and beloved Son of God is revealed to his inner circle of friends. Picture Peter, in the midst of his impulsive activism, suddenly silenced by the overpowering reality of the presence of God.

Scripture Meditation: Matthew 17:2

And he was transfigured before them, and his face shone like the sun, and his clothes became dazzling white.

Enter into this vision of Jesus as experienced by Peter, James, and John. Sing the first verse of the song. See yourself surrounded by the light of Christ's presence.

Reflecting in Song

The ability to have a vision is part of what it means to be human. Through vision, which is closely tied to imagination, God has blessed us with the capacity to transcend the physical reality of the moment. Most of us have many different visions, and we live our lives accordingly. We may envision a beautiful new home, so we go to work each day in order to make it a reality. Or we envision an exciting career, so we get an education and seek out those who can help bring it to pass. Without a vision an artist cannot create. Our visions motivate us and drive us—whether it be for good or evil, for God or self. They also influence our emotional states. They can cause fear and depression, or they can bring peace and joy.

No doubt the disciples were feeling fear and depression just before God blessed them with this vision of Christ's true glory. They had recently heard sobering words from Jesus' mouth—words about his crucifixion and about losing their own lives. The transfiguration provided the vision for them to persevere through the dark days of Calvary and the hardships they encountered in preaching the gospel.

This song is a paraphrase of an ancient Irish poem. It is a prayer to Christ that we might see him as he truly is and that this vision might be the supreme motivation of our lives.

Pray slowly through the verses of the hymn. It is an intensely personal prayer, centering on all that Christ is. Reflect on who he is. He is everything from the transcendent High King of heaven to the immanently personal Bridegroom. His roles as Savior, Teacher, Lord, and Friend, along with many others, are included here.

Scripture tells us that "Christ is all and in all" (Col. 3:11). This song asks, "All that you are, may you be to me." Sing the song through. May Christ be all of this, and more, to you.

Questions of Examen and Exercises of Devotion

1. What visions are currently motivating my life?
2. Do any of these visions interfere with my vision of Christ?
3. Verse four is a prayer of protection. Sing it each day for a week as you put on "the whole armor of God" (Eph. 6:11).
4. Pray different verses of this hymn for friends or loved ones as you perceive their needs and as the Spirit leads. ("Be thou her Wisdom. . . .")

The Prayer of the Heart

Lord, let me see the flaming reality of your splendor and holiness, your love and mercy. Let this vision fill me and be the driving force of my life. I give you all my other visions and dreams, thoughts and ideas and ask that they be brought into clearer focus with you. Amen.

Stay with Me

Words from Matthew 26   Jacques Berthier

Ostinato Chorale

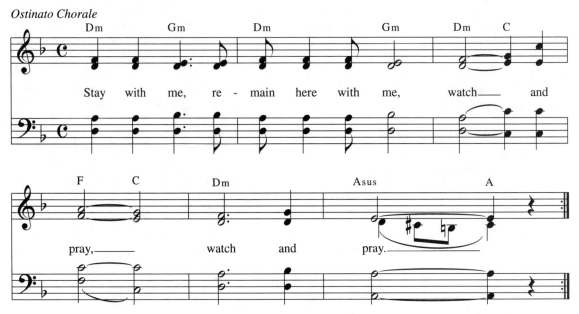

Stay with me, re - main here with me, watch____ and pray,____ watch and pray.____

Scripture Reading: Matthew 26:30–56

Read this passage and relive the events of the night before Jesus' crucifixion. Hear the disciples, led by Peter, emphatically assuring Jesus that they will stay with him no matter what. Follow Jesus into the garden of Gethsemane, through his struggle in prayer, and then his betrayal and arrest. And finally, see all of Jesus' friends running away, leaving him alone to face torture, suffering, and death.

Scripture Meditation: Matthew 26:38

"I am deeply grieved, even to death; remain here, and stay awake with me."

Enter into this intimate scene as Jesus, in the midst of excruciating agony of heart and mind, pleads in vain with Peter, James, and John to stay awake with him. Repeat these words of Jesus. Think of times of distress in your own life when you have felt the need of human companionship and support. Scripture tells us Jesus had the same human needs that we feel (Heb. 2:17). Identify with his pain and isolation, and thank him for suffering this for you. Give him your loving companionship now.

Reflecting in Song

This meditative chorale, echoing the words of Jesus, comes from the Taizé tradition. The Taizé Community is an international, ecumenical fellowship whose chief work is prayer and worship. Located in France, it is made up of brothers of many nationalities from both Protestant and Catholic denominations who have committed themselves to celibacy and life together. Visitors from around the world come to Taizé to enter into worship, participate in retreats, and discover ways to live out their own lives of prayer and commitment.

Over the past two decades an entire body of simple, liturgical song has been developed by the Taizé Community. Taizé songs are sung in many languages and have become known worldwide. Often the songs contain a refrain or response to be sung quietly and repeatedly (*ostinato*) by the congregation while a cantor sings solo verses of scriptural or liturgical texts. These simple refrains and responses lead into the prayer of the heart; the words go ever deeper into one until the heart is praying without ceasing. Sing through this song. Repeat it until it is familiar. Now read and contemplate these words of Jesus as taken from the Scripture passage. Pause and sing the song in response as indicated (R).

> *"Sit here while I go over there and pray." (R)*
> *"I am deeply grieved, even to death; remain here, and stay awake with me." (R)*
> *"My Father, if it is possible, let this cup pass from me; yet not what I want but what you want." (R)*
> *"So, could you not stay awake with me one hour? Stay awake and pray that you may not come into the time of trial; the spirit indeed is willing, but the flesh is weak." (R)*
> *"My Father, if this cannot pass unless I drink it, your will be done." (R)*

Sometimes it is difficult to read these words because we identify so closely with disciples. We sleep in apathy or we run away in fear, leaving Jesus to suffer alone. But we must not forget the rest of the story. As he did with the disciples, Jesus forgives us and welcomes us back. He loves us. He trusts us to take his message to the world. And he promises, "I am with you always" (Matt. 28:20).

Questions of Examen and Exercises of Devotion

1. Have I on any occasion deserted Jesus out of fear (or deserted anyone else—"As you do it to the least of these, you do it to me")?
2. Have I on any occasion stayed with Jesus despite fear (or stayed with someone else, in Jesus' name)?
3. Sing this song each morning for one week. Let it be as the voice of Jesus calling you back into his presence, back to his side.
4. One ancient Christian practice is "watchings," going without sleep for extended times of prayer and worship. Experience a one-night watch from, say, 10:00 P.M. until 6:00 A.M.—eight hours. You may want to plan some of the time with set liturgies and allow other parts of the time to be more open-ended. (One musician played sacred music on the piano throughout the night to prepare himself for a sunrise watch on a hilltop.)

The Prayer of the Heart

Lord, too many times I let you down, or I run away. Have mercy. Forgive. Help me to watch and pray. Amen.

O Sacred Head, Now Wounded

Attr. to Bernard of Clairvaux, 12th C.
Tr. (German) Paul Gerhardt, 1656
Tr. (English) James W. Alexander, 1830

PASSION CHORALE (7.6.7.6.D.)
Hans Leo Hassler, 1601

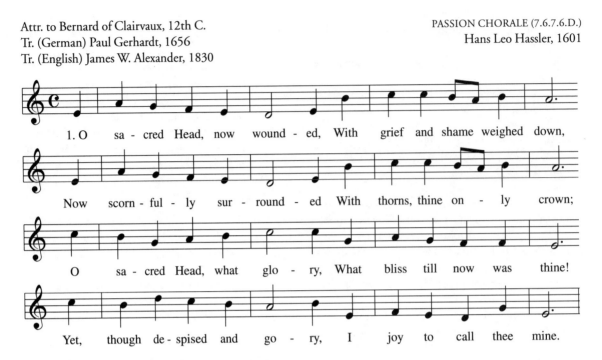

1. O sacred Head, now wounded, With grief and shame weighed down,
Now scornfully surrounded With thorns, thine only crown;
O sacred Head, what glory, What bliss till now was thine!
Yet, though despised and gory, I joy to call thee mine.

2. What thou, my Lord, hast suffered
Was all for sinners' gain;
Mine, mine was the transgression,
But thine the deadly pain.
Lo, here I fall, my Savior!
'Tis I deserve thy place;
Look on me with thy favor,
And grant to me thy grace.

3. What language shall I borrow
To thank thee, dearest friend,
For this thy dying sorrow,
Thy pity without end?
O make me thine forever;
And should I fainting be,
Lord, let me never, never
Outlive my love to thee.

Scripture Reading:
Matthew 27:27–31, Isaiah 53:3–6

In reading these Scriptures side by side, it is amazing to realize the graphic accuracy with which the prophet Isaiah predicts and describes Jesus' sufferings and death. Recall that Matthew has previously identified Jesus with the Suffering Servant referred to in Isaiah 53 (see Matt. 8:17).

Scripture Meditation: Isaiah 53:5 (RSV)

But he was wounded for our transgressions,
he was bruised for our iniquities;

upon him was the chastisement that made us whole,
and with his stripes we are healed.

Think on these lines. Personalize them, and pray them. ("You were wounded for *my* transgressions. . . .") Read and pray through the hymn, pausing after each verse to repeat this Scripture from Isaiah.

Reflecting in Song

This beautiful, classic hymn set to a German chorale tune is a translation of part of a medieval Latin poem traditionally ascribed to Bernard of Clairvaux. The poem addresses the various parts of Christ's body as they hang on the cross.

Contemplation of pain and suffering was common in medieval times with attention given to graphic detail. Meditation on the wounds of Christ was an accepted form of Lenten devotion and was sometimes looked upon as a way of earning favor with God. It may seem to us that Christians in the Middle Ages were misguided in their motivation and mistaken in emphasizing suffering to such a degree. But perhaps we in our culture have erred in the opposite direction. Purposeful meditation on pain and suffering seems offensive and unhealthy to us. True, we are inundated with violence and suffering in the media, but it is depicted in an artless, detached manner. It is presented either as impersonal news quickly interrupted by a commercial or as entertainment to be viewed while munching popcorn. Rather than entering into the victim's pain, we become desensitized. And we strive at all costs to avoid personal pain and suffering or any thought of it.

With this as with all of the spiritual disciplines, it is easy to find ourselves out of balance. The Church has always tended to swing from one extreme to another, just as we tend to do in our own lives. We must strive for balance between the excesses of the Middle Ages and the neglect of our age.

The writer to the Hebrews says, "Consider him who endured such hostility against himself from sinners, so that you may not grow weary and lose heart" (Heb. 12:3). Through meditating on the sufferings of Christ, we are able to enter into his pain not as a means of earning favor with God or doing "penance" but in order that we "may know him and the power of his resurrection, and may share his sufferings" (Phil. 3:10). When I share his pain, I am drawn into Christ's wounded, bleeding heart of love, and I identify with the pain of a wounded, bleeding world through which he still suffers. Sing the first verse of the hymn, and share in the sufferings of Christ.

As I share in his pain, I realize that it is my sin and no one else's that is the cause of Jesus' sufferings. Luther, in his "Meditation on Christ's Passion," wrote, "The real and true work of Christ's passion is to make man conformable to Christ."[2] We meditate upon his suffering in order that we might become holy. But, Luther cautions, "You must first seek God's grace and ask that it be accomplished by his grace and not by your own power." Sing the second verse. Ask that God's work of grace be done in your heart.

After we have meditated on the pain and suffering of Christ, Luther exhorts us to watch that sin does not settle in our conscience. In faith we cast our sins on Christ, knowing that they are forgiven. Then we move past his sufferings, seeing his "friendly heart and how this heart beats with such love for you." Continuing on, we "rise beyond Christ's heart to God's heart," the heart of the Father who loved us so that he gave his only Son. Sing the last verse of the hymn. Worship and give thanks. Offer yourself to Christ in response to his undying love for you.

Questions of Examen and Exercises of Devotion

1. What sin in my heart is causing Christ to suffer?
2. Can I cast this upon him, knowing it is really forgiven?
3. Read and reflect upon Luther's "Meditation on Christ's Passion." It is available from the source listed in the endnotes.
4. J. S. Bach made use of this chorale in his *Passion According to St. Matthew.* Check out a recording and follow Bach's musical setting of Matthew 26–27. (Note: It is available in both German and English editions.)

The Prayer of the Heart

Lord Jesus, when I consider your sufferings and see what my sin has done, I am crushed. When I see the love you have poured out for me, I am overwhelmed. I give you thanks and praise, but my words are insufficient, Lord. May my life speak forth your glory and mirror your sacrificial love. Amen.

In the Garden

GARDEN (Irregular)

C. Austin Miles, 1912

C. Austin Miles, 1912

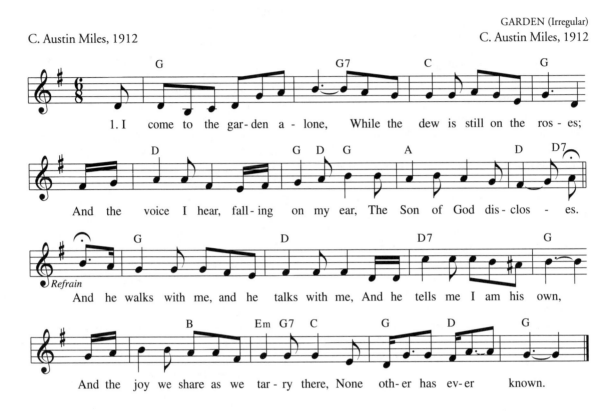

1. I come to the gar-den a - lone, While the dew is still on the ros - es;
And the voice I hear, fall-ing on my ear, The Son of God dis - clos - es.

Refrain

And he walks with me, and he talks with me, And he tells me I am his own,

And the joy we share as we tar - ry there, None oth-er has ev-er known.

2. He speaks, and the sound of his voice
   Is so sweet the birds hush their singing;
   And the melody that he gave to me
   Within my heart is ringing.

3. I'd stay in the garden with him
   Though the night around me be falling;
   But he bids me go; through the voice of woe,
   His voice to me is calling.

Scripture Reading: John 19:41–20:18

In this, John's account of the resurrection of Jesus, follow Mary Magdalene and two of the disciples as they discover the empty tomb. See Mary, staying in the garden after the others have left, weeping and seeking her Lord.

Scripture Meditation: John 20:16

Jesus said to her, "Mary!" She turned and said to him in Hebrew, "Rabboni!" (which means Teacher).

As you meditate on the Scripture, experience with Mary the amazement and joy of this encounter. She is the first person to meet the crucified and risen Lord face to face. Here is joy that "none other has ever known." Sing the first verse of the song and enter into Mary's joy.

Reflecting in Song

It was following a time of profound meditation on these verses from John (during which he witnessed in a vision the drama of this moment in Mary's life) that C. Austin Miles wrote "In the Garden." The song has been a favorite and a mainstay of evangelical hymnody ever since.

In her book, *The Secret Garden of the Soul*, written around the same time as this hymn, Presbyterian journalist Emily Herman says, "Every soul that is truly alive has a garden of which no other holds the key," a place "where Jesus walks with His disciples, and the clash of the world cannot drown the music of His voice." She notes that we, his disciples, have always tended to give that garden either far more or far less than its true place and that the key to a "perfectly balanced Christian character is found in its attitude toward that secret garden of the soul's delight."[3]

God desires to meet each of us in the garden. He enjoys our companionship and fellowship. The Lord God walked in the Garden of Eden in the cool of the day, seeking the company of the man and woman he had made. But he found to his great sorrow that the fellowship had been broken—by Adam and Eve's own choice. Still, he patiently sought them and bought them back at a tremendous cost. In the person of his only Son, the fellowship of the garden has been restored. Sing the first verse of "In the Garden" again. Meet the risen Lord there, knowing that he delights in your company. *The Garden of Jesus*, a seventeenth-century

Dutch poem, pictures Jesus as the Gardener of our hearts. Realize how much pleasure he takes in the flowers and fruits of his Spirit growing in your heart.

The garden not only brings joy to the Gardener; it is for our enjoyment as well. Filled with vibrant color, gentle fragrance, and the music of birds, it enchants our senses. And our "fairest Lord Jesus" whom we meet there is even more beautiful. His song is infinitely sweeter. Sing the second verse. Enjoy the refreshment of the garden and the beauty of his presence. Let him sing his song into your heart.

The garden is a place of peace and rest, but it is also a place of life and growth. It shelters us and prepares us to go forth and bear fruit in the world. After precious times in the garden with his Father, Jesus went out, living his life amid the noise, filth, and hostility of the crowds. In the garden he received strength and health to minister to the sick and the wounded, the lost and the sorrowing. Theirs is the "voice of woe" through which we perceive his voice. He calls us to come with him out of the garden and bring life and beauty into a hurting, dying world. Sing the third verse. Listen, and consider where he might be calling you today.

Questions of Examen and Exercises of Devotion

1. What fruits and flowers are there in my life to bring joy to the Gardener?
2. Is there any sin that like Adam and Eve's hinders my fellowship with the Lord in the garden?
3. Reflect on the garden references in these Scriptures: Song of Solomon 6:2–3; Isaiah 58:6–11, 61:10–11; Jeremiah 31:10–12.
4. Enjoy the beauty of a local garden, and spend some time alone with the Gardener of your soul.

The Prayer of the Heart

Lord, so many times I leave you waiting in the garden. Forgive me. Help me sense your presence and meet you there often. May I give the garden its rightful place, and may I carry its beauty, fragrance, and song out into the world. Amen.

Jesus, I Am Resting, Resting

TRANQUILITY (8.7.8.5.D. with refrain)

Jean S. Pigott, 1876

James Mountain, 1876

1. Je - sus, I am rest - ing, rest - ing In the joy of what Thou art;
2. O, how great Thy lov - ing kind - ness, Vast - er, broad - er than the sea!
3. Sim - ply trust - ing Thee, Lord Je - sus, I be - hold Thee as Thou art,
4. Ev - er lift Thy face up - on me As I work and wait for Thee;
(Ref.) Je - sus, I am rest - ing, rest - ing In the joy of what Thou art;

Fine

I am find - ing out the great - ness Of Thy lov - ing heart.
O, how mar - vel - ous Thy good - ness, Lav - ished all on me!
And Thy love, so pure, so change - less, Sat - is - fies my heart;
Rest - ing 'neath Thy smile, Lord Je - sus, Earth's dark shad - ows flee.
I am find - ing out the great - ness Of Thy lov - ing heart.

Thou hast bid me gaze up - on Thee, And Thy beau - ty fills my soul,
Yes, I rest in Thee, Be - lov - ed, Know what wealth of grace is Thine,
Sat - is - fies its deep - est long - ings, Meets, sup - plies its ev - ery need,
Bright - ness of my Fa - ther's glo - ry, Sun - shine of my Fa - ther's face,

D.C. Refrain

For by Thy trans - form - ing pow - er, Thou hast made me whole.
Know Thy cer - tain - ty of prom - ise, And have made it mine.
Com - pass - eth me round with bless - ings: Thine is love in - deed!
Keep me ev - er trust - ing, rest - ing, Fill me with Thy grace.

Scripture Reading: Isaiah 30:15–21

While reading this passage, be attentive to the call of the prophet Isaiah to rest and trust. This call is echoed throughout Scripture, and it is the same call to us today. Notice how self-reliant activism brings only panic and fear to Judah. But God patiently stays with his rebellious people. The promised Teacher is waiting for his children to return. And he waits for us too.

Scripture Meditation: Isaiah 30:15

In returning and rest you shall be saved;
in quietness and in trust shall be your strength.

Be still before God, allowing these words to sink into your heart. Spend some time in quietness. Then sing the refrain of this song. Sing it again, this time from memory. The refrain speaks of two contrasting actions—resting and finding out. Enjoy both the peaceful rest and the exciting freedom of discovery available in Christ's great heart of love.

Reflecting in Song

Augustine writes, "You have made us for yourself, and our heart is restless until it rests in You."[4] Jesus wants to put our hearts at rest not just when we first meet him but daily and experientially throughout our lives. Meditating on this hymn can help lead us into his rest. Read the verses as indicated below, pausing often and singing the refrain after each verse. The refrain, especially when sung from memory, offers the benefit of repetition and gives the verses a chance to soak in.

Turn your attention to verse one. Realize that it is not simply a passive rest we are entering into. It is a transforming rest, for we become like those we spend time with and admire. Rest, then, in Jesus as you grow into his likeness.

In reading verse two, call to mind the wealth of grace and loving-kindness you have in Christ. John Calvin tells us that a godly mind is not formed by precepts and sanctions so much as by "a serious meditation on the Divine goodness towards it."[5] Rest and meditate on the divine goodness of the Beloved.

Verse three reminds us that only Jesus can satisfy the deepest longings of our hearts. We may have physical and mental rest, but unless we have spiritual rest, our rest is incomplete. So now, rest and let Jesus speak to the desires of your heart.

Not until the last verse do we find any requests in this prayer. The first three verses have focused on love and adoration. But in verse four we are drawn into supplication, asking for grace to work and wait, trust and rest. Jesus promises, "Come to me, all you that are weary and are carrying heavy burdens, and I will give you rest" (Matt. 11:28). Rest in the assurance that your request is granted.

Prayerfully sing the entire song. Hum the refrain after each verse instead of singing the words. Use this as a type of *Selah,* the meditative interlude found in the Psalms, and let the verses continue ministering to your heart.

Questions of Examen and Exercises of Devotion

1. What aspect of the heart of Jesus have I discovered recently?
2. What obstacles hinder my daily rest in Christ?
3. Consider making this hymn along with some related Scriptures the theme for a personal retreat.
4. Next time you meet an unexpected delay or period of waiting, make it a time of rest and "meditation on the divine goodness."

The Prayer of the Heart

Jesus, I long to rest in your loving heart and to know you better. I confess the busyness and preoccupation that keep me from you. Calm my heart that I may hear your voice and respond in joy to your invitation to rest and peace, quietness and trust. Amen.

Precious Lord, Take My Hand

PRECIOUS LORD (6.6.9.6.6.9.)

Thomas A. Dorsey, 1938

George N. Allen, 1844, Adapt. by Thomas A. Dorsey, 1938

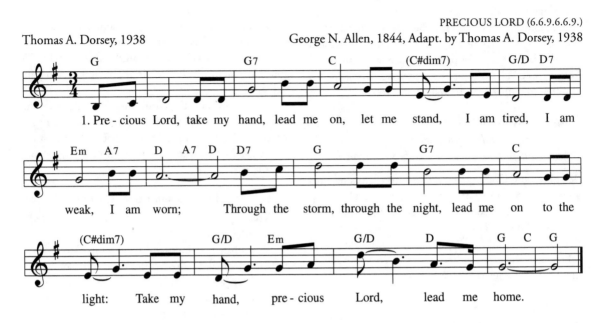

1. Pre - cious Lord, take my hand, lead me on, let me stand, I am tired, I am weak, I am worn; Through the storm, through the night, lead me on to the light: Take my hand, pre - cious Lord, lead me home.

2. When my way grows drear, precious Lord, linger near,
When my life is almost gone;
Hear my cry, hear my call, hold my hand lest I fall:
Take my hand, precious Lord, lead me home.

3. When the darkness appears and the night draws near,
And the day is past and gone,
At the river I stand, guide my feet, hold my hand:
Take my hand, precious Lord, lead me home.

Scripture Reading: Psalm 23

Repeat from memory as much of this well-known psalm as you are able. Now read it. Give attention to the Shepherd who leads and guides, protects and provides. He not only meets needs, he supplies overflowing blessings. He gives life, abundantly. Call to mind the words of Jesus: "I am the good shepherd. The good shepherd lays down his life for the sheep" (John 10:11).

Scripture Meditation: Psalm 23:4 (KJV)

> *Yea, though I walk through the valley of the shadow of death, I will fear no evil: for thou art with me; thy rod and thy staff they comfort me.*

As you consider this Scripture, think of what the "valley of the shadow" is for you. Maybe it is loneliness, weariness, or turmoil. Maybe it is illness or the fear of death. Having faced your valley, dwell on this certainty: the Good Shepherd is with you. Even when it is too dark to see him, know that his rod will guide you, his staff will protect you. Let this be your comfort.

Reflecting in Song

This song is the heart cry of one who understood the valley of the shadow of death. Thomas A. Dorsey penned this prayer song in 1932 following the death of his wife and infant son. In the first verse we see a person who has reached the end of his resources: "I am tired, I am weak, I am worn." It is the heart cry of a weary, frightened child—every weary, frightened child. As you sing the first verse, consider ways in which you are weary and frightened.

Thomas Dorsey, the "Father of Gospel Music," was a well-known blues and jazz pianist in his youth. Experiencing a serious illness in his midtwenties moved him to turn his talents exclusively toward sacred music. He brought to the spirituals and hymns of his childhood "the feelings and the pathos and moans of the blues," thus becoming the originator of black Gospel music.[6]

Improvisation on the melody is inherent to the Gospel style just as it was to the Baroque style of Handel and Bach. Improvising allows the Spirit to move in our music, giving a uniqueness and personality to each "incarnation" of a song. This is the beauty of Gospel music. Sing the second and third verses. Do not rush the tempo. Improvise freely as the words move you and as the Spirit leads you.

For days after the death of his wife and child, Dorsey was lost in grief and unable to play or sing. "I felt that God had done me an injustice," he said. "I didn't want to serve him anymore or write gospel songs. I just wanted to go back to that jazz world I once knew so well."[7] A friend encouraged him to sit down at the piano. He played and sought comfort in hymns, and it was his improvisation on George N. Allan's tune MAITLAND ("Must Jesus Bear the Cross Alone?") that inspired the words and music to "Precious Lord, Take My Hand."

Sing the song once again. As you are able, let go of your struggle to "hold on" and invite the "precious Lord" to take your hand. A child who struggles is much harder to lead than one who surrenders and trusts. Let go, and let him lead you safely home.

Questions of Examen and Exercises of Devotion

1. Through what darkness is the Shepherd leading me?
2. Are there times I have refused to let God take my hand?
3. Memorize or review your memorization of Psalm 23.
4. For one month allow "Precious Lord, Take My Hand" to be the first words of the morning and the last words of the evening. Keep journal notations on what you learn from the experience.

The Prayer of the Heart

Precious Lord, faithful Shepherd, whether in meadows of the brightest light or valleys of the darkest night, may your loving grip hold me secure. Amen.

Come Home
(The Father's Invitation)

Miriam Overholt   Miriam Overholt

5- bar interlude in accompaniment

© 1994 Miriam Kline Overholt

Accompaniment for this song is found on page 130.

Scripture Reading: Luke 15:11–32

Jesus told this parable of the lost son as the culmination of three parables dealing with the lost and the found. Two sons are portrayed here—one prodigal and self-indulgent, one frugal and obedient. Read and consider the ways in which each son was, in fact, lost. Picture the brothers' relationship with each other. See how the father's loving heart embraces them both.

Scripture Meditation: Luke 15:20

> *But while he was still far off, his father saw him and was filled with compassion; he ran and put his arms around him and kissed him.*

As you contemplate this Scripture, imagine yourself in the place of the father. You have assumed your younger son to be dead, yet you have held to a thread of hope, constantly waiting and watching for news of him. One day, far off in the distance, you see a broken but unmistakable form coming toward you. Experience the emotion in the father's heart. Read through the words of this song.

Reflecting in Song

The love of an earthly father for his sons is but a shadow of the love our heavenly Father has for each of us. God "aches over our distance and preoccupation. He mourns that we do not draw near to him. . . . He longs for our presence. And he is inviting you—and me—to come home, to come home to where we belong, to come home to that for which we were created. His arms are stretched out wide to receive us. His heart is enlarged to take us in."[8]

It was after reading these words in *Prayer: Finding the Heart's True Home* that Miriam Overholt wrote the song "Come Home." She relates, "So often I stand outside of God's accepting welcome because of my fears and insecurities. I tell myself that I am not good enough or smart enough or talented enough to be pleasing to God. But that is not what he says. He says, 'Come home.'"

Some of us are like the younger brother. We have rejected our Father, lived in rebellion, and squandered his gifts. We have run away from home. And some of us are like the elder brother. We have served faithfully and obediently but with self-righteousness and judg-ment, bitterness and unforgiveness. We live away from home without realizing it.

In the parable we know that the younger son decided to come home. But we're not told what the elder son finally did. It may have been harder for him to "come home" because he had to first admit that he'd been "away." To come home also meant he would have to be reconciled with his brother, who he felt had gotten what rightfully belonged to him and whom he could only refer to as "this son of yours." As the story closes, the father continues his loving entreaty.

In the same way, God continues to call each of us home—"home to serenity and peace and joy, home to friendship and fellowship and openness, home to intimacy and acceptance and affirmation."[9]

Scripture tells us that God is singing over us (Zeph. 3:17). Sing this song, and listen. This is a love song—the song of a father to his child. It is a song of invitation. It is the song God is singing to you at this very moment. Respond to his voice.

Questions of Examen and Exercises of Devotion

1. In what ways do I identify with either or both of the sons in the parable?
2. What fears, insecurities, or unbeliefs keep me from responding to God's welcoming invitation?
3. We cannot live peacefully at home if we are estranged from someone else in the family. Is there anyone with whom you need reconciliation? If so, set a plan for reconciling.
4. If you feel yourself to be like the brother who stayed at home but who knew estrangement nonetheless, write down three actions you can do that will begin the process of restoring your first love.

The Prayer of the Heart

O God, my God, I know I am never fully home until I make my home in you. Thank you for the welcome mat. Amen.

Like a River Glorious

WYE VALLEY (6.5.6.5.D. with refrain)

Frances R. Havergal, 1874

James Mountain, 1876

1. Like a riv-er glo-rious is God's per-fect peace, o-ver all vic-to-rious
2. Hid-den in the hol-low of his bless-ed hand, nev-er foe can fol-low,
3. Ev-ery joy or tri-al fall-eth from a-bove, traced up-on our di-al

in its bright in-crease; Per-fect, yet it flow-eth full-er ev-ery day,
nev-er trai-tor stand; Not a surge of wor-ry, not a shade of care,
by the Sun of Love; We may trust him ful-ly all for us to do;

Refrain

per-fect, yet it grow-eth deep-er all the way. Stayed up-on Je-ho-vah,
not a blast of hur-ry touch the spir-it there.
they who trust him whol-ly find him whol-ly true.

hearts are ful-ly blest, Find-ing, as he prom-ised, per-fect peace and rest.

Scripture Reading: Isaiah 26:1–12

Amid pronouncements of judgment and predictions of impending doom, Isaiah always draws the reader back to the goodness and faithfulness of God. In this passage he does it by means of a song. While reading this ancient song, note that God is the one who brings judgment, gives salvation, and ordains peace. The role of God's people is one of trusting, waiting, seeking.

Scripture Meditation: Isaiah 26:3 (KJV)

Thou wilt keep him in perfect peace, whose mind is stayed on thee: because he trusteth in thee.

Close your eyes and repeat this Scripture text several times. Meditate on the person of God. Hear his words: "Be still, and know that I am God" (Ps. 46:10). Speak affirmations of God's character—affirmations like "Wonderful Counselor," "Mighty God," "Everlasting Father." Meditate on the Prince of Peace, and see him saying to the waves, "Peace, be still." Ask him to calm the waves in your mind and spirit. Accept the peace of God, which goes deeper than all human understanding.

Reflecting in Song

This hymn likens the peace of God to a mighty river. God's peace, in others words, is not a shallow, static peace. It is a deep, dynamic, and growing peace—overwhelming, flooding, clearing every obstacle from its path. Just as a river can be recognized from a considerable distance by the abundant life growing up all around it, so it is with God's peace. New life springs up wherever this *shalom* of God flows. *Shalom,* far more than just the absence of strife, is the presence of healing and wholeness, harmony and fulfillment. Sing the first verse of the hymn. Let the *shalom* of God flood your soul.

Read the first verse again, noting the use of the word *perfect.* In the Hebrew text the phrase translated "perfect peace" reads "*shalom shalom.*" Repetition of the word indicates intensity, completeness, perfection. Frances Ridley Havergal, the young woman who wrote this song, memorized the entire book of Isaiah and was proficient in Hebrew. She studied the Hebrew Scriptures regularly so knew well the meaning of this text when she wrote of "God's perfect peace." Think on the perfection of God's peace in contrast to that of human society.

Turn your attention to the refrain. Sing it and see how it mirrors the Scripture verse. Where the song speaks of the heart stayed upon Jehovah, the English version uses the term *mind.* In Hebrew this word actually means "imagination"—a word sometimes viewed with suspicion in relation to the spiritual life. But consider for a moment: does not much of what robs us of peace arise from our imaginations? The what-ifs and the if-onlys—scenes of future fears or past failures that seem to spring up in our minds automatically—create anxiety and worry, depression and despair. But the imagination grounded in the Word, centered on God, and inspired by his Spirit is a source of peace and joy, security and confidence. We need not fear imagining or expecting too much of God, for he is "able to accomplish abundantly far more than all we can ask or imagine" (Eph. 3:20).

Sing the last two verses of the song. Appreciate the security, the calm assurance, the absolute trust that is expressed. Frances Ridley Havergal had this assurance in her heart. At the age of forty-two she was told she had only a short time to live. Frances responded, "If I am really going, it is too good to be true!" She died soon afterward while singing a hymn, "Jesus, I Will Trust Thee." Hers was the peace that this world cannot give—the perfect *shalom* of God. It is a "perfect peace" that can be ours as well.

Questions of Examen and Exercises of Devotion

1. Are any what-ifs or if-onlys hindering the peace of God in my life? Can I give them over to him?
2. What specific thing can I do this week to help center my mind on God?
3. Notice during the coming week the role your imagination plays in any fear, anxiety, or depression you may experience. Pause and give your thoughts to God. Hear the words of Jesus: "Peace, be still."
4. River imagery runs throughout the Bible: Genesis 2:10–14; Psalm 1:1–3, 42:1–2, 46:4–5; Isaiah 33:20–22, 41:17–20; John 7:37–39; Revelation 22:1–5. Read and focus on the river's associations with life, peace, and prosperity.

The Prayer of the Heart

O God, River glorious, flood me with your peace. I give you my mind, my imagination, my heart. May they ever be steadfast in you. Amen.

Songs of Holiness

The absolute test of valid religious experience is . . . in the vivid
sense of the need for purification, the sense that something has got
to be done *to* us and won't be done until we see our condition
as it really is and ask to be cleansed of it.

—*Evelyn Underhill*

The nearer we come to the light of God's love, the fuller our contrition at
our distance from God and our preoccupation with ourselves. Exposure
to the light leads us to confession, and walking in the light leads us to
fellowship (1 John 1:7). This ongoing fellowship with Christ and his people, in its time and in its way, will form us, conform us, and transform
us into the image of Christ (Gal. 4:19; Rom. 8:29, 12:2).

This process, however, is not easy, nor is it uninterrupted progress
forward. Real effort is needed; we "strive to enter in," as Jesus tells us.
Remember, the opposite of grace is works, not effort. Works has to do
with merit; God's grace is unearned and unearnable. Effort, on the other
hand, has to do with our cooperation with the grace of God operating
in our lives.

And in our efforts we will experience plenty of backtracking and false
starts and reversals. This is the way we grow in anything. (Remember, we
are not so much looking for perfection as for progress.) When this happens—and it will happen—we pray again, *Kyrie eleison,* "Lord, have
mercy." And we take up the journey once more, learning, ever learning,
to "Trust and obey, for there's no other way to be happy in Jesus, but to
trust and obey."

Come, Ye Sinners, Poor and Needy

ARISE (8.7.8.7. with refrain)

Joseph Hart, 1759 (refrain, anonymous)

Early American Folk Melody, from *Southern Harmony* (1835)

1. Come, ye sin - ners, poor and need - y, weak and wound - ed, sick and sore;
2. Come, ye thirst - y, come, and wel - come, God's free boun - ty glo - ri - fy;
3. Come, ye wea - ry, heav - y la - den, lost and ru - ined by the fall;
4. Let not con - science make you lin - ger, nor of fit - ness fond - ly dream;

Je - sus read - y stands to save you, full of pit - y, love, and pow'r.
True be - lief and true re - pent - ance, ev - ery grace that brings you nigh.
If you tar - ry till you're bet - ter, you will nev - er come at all.
All the fit - ness he re - quir - eth is to feel your need of him.

Refrain

I will a - rise and go to Je - sus; he will em - brace me in his arms;

In the arms of my dear Sav - ior, O, there are ten thou - sand charms.

Scripture Reading: Mark 2:13–17

As you read this, picture the crowds milling about Jesus, hanging on his every word. See Levi (also known as Matthew) the tax collector, the object of everyone's scorn and derision, looking on from a distance. Imagine his reaction when Jesus approached and said, "Follow me." It didn't take him long to make up his mind. Now, sing the first verse of this song and put yourself in Levi's place.

Scripture Meditation: Mark 2:17

Those who are well have no need of a physician, but those who are sick; I have come to call not the righteous but sinners.

After reflecting on these words of Jesus, read through the hymn. Notice the many different needs named in it and God's abundant provision for each one. Be sensitive to any need you might have, and give it to Jesus. Thank him for publicly befriending the "poor and needy."

Reflecting in Song

Most of us will not turn to God until we really need him. We seldom come when we're rich and satisfied. As British statesman William Wilberforce observed, "Prosperity hardens the heart."[1] Have you heard many testimonies such as, "I won the lottery and I was so thankful, I gave my life to Jesus"? Or maybe, "I had a wonderful wife, healthy kids, a home and a great job. I came to God out of gratitude." No. More often it is pain, suffering, or hardship that brings us to him. We are driven to God by our need rather than turning to him freely out of love and thankfulness.

This was certainly the case with the Israelites. Time and time again after God had blessed them with peace and prosperity, they would forget him and turn to idols. When they sank in sin to the point of despair, they would cry out, and he would save them once again. And this pattern is often played out in our own lives.

The life of Joseph Hart, an eighteenth-century English minister and author of this hymn, was no different. He wrote of his early attempts to make himself a Christian by practicing "mere doctrine" and adopting the opinions of others. In the name of Christian liberty he spent years in a state of carnality and wickedness. When he tried to reform himself, he failed, admitting, "the fountains of the great deeps of my sinful nature were not broken up."

Eventually he fell into a serious depression that was aggravated by pain and physical illness. In this condition late in life his heart was finally softened. He said it "made me fling myself on my knees before God."[2] Joseph Hart knew what it meant to come to Christ in poverty and need.

Our heavenly Father hurts along with us when we come to the point of despair. He grieves with us when we suffer. "God's kindness is meant to lead you to repentance," Paul reminds us (Rom. 2:4). But we continue to presume upon his kindness, forbearance, and patience. So he waits and then welcomes us in our despair and our need. He sends his only Son with a special invitation. As you sing this song, respond to this grace-filled invitation.

Questions of Examen and Exercises of Devotion

1. Have I, like the Pharisees in the Scripture, at times judged others for their association with someone "undesirable"?
2. In what ways might the pattern of my life resemble the pattern exhibited by the Israelites?
3. Think of times of particular need when Christ met you in the past. Thank him for being there.
4. Jean Vanier, founder of L'Arche Communities, says that God comes to the little and the wounded and to each of us to the extent that we accept that we are little and wounded. Write out five ways you see yourself as little and wounded before God.

The Prayer of the Heart

Lord Jesus, I confess I have presumed upon your patience and loving-kindness. I come to you, "weak and wounded, sick and sore." I come, once again, in poverty and in need. Thank you that this is all you ask. Amen.

Kyrie Eleison
(Lord, Have Mercy)
Setting 1

Ancient Greek text

Janet L. Janzen

In quiet reflection

Ky - ri - e e - le - i - son, Chris - te e - le - i - son, Ky - ri - e e -

lei - son, e - le - i - son. son.

© 1993, Janet Lindeblad Janzen

Setting 2

Swedish Melody
From "Bjuråkers Handskrift," prior to 1550

Ky - ri - e e - le - i - son, Ky - ri - e e - le - i - son.

The third setting of the *Kyrie* is found on page 133.

Scripture Reading: Luke 18:9–14

Jesus targets a specific audience when he tells this parable of the Pharisee and the tax collector. Notice to whom he is speaking, and imagine yourself a part of that audience. Read the passage again and put yourself in the place of the Pharisee, then of the tax collector. Compare their prayers. Think about ways you identify with these two people.

Scripture Meditation: Luke 18:13

But the tax collector, standing far off, would not even look up to heaven, but was beating his breast and saying, "God, be merciful to me, a sinner!"

Enter into this prayer of contrition. See how the tax collector expresses himself physically and emotionally as well as spiritually as he throws himself on the mercy of God. Seek this gift of heartfelt repentance.

Reflecting in Song

The mercy of God forms a continuous theme throughout Scripture. God's covenant with the children of Israel was an act of mercy. And though they proved unfaithful, "Yet he, being compassionate, forgave their iniquity and did not destroy them" (Ps. 78:38). The cry for mercy, echoing throughout the Psalter, was a part of Hebrew worship.

In the fullness of time God's ultimate expression of mercy was shown in the sacrifice of his Son. Early Christians included this penitential prayer, *Kyrie eleison,* in their worship. Pope Gregory incorporated the *Kyrie* into the standardized liturgy of the Western Church in the sixth century, adding the phrase *Christe eleison* ("Christ, have mercy"). Since then it has continued to be used in liturgical churches in one form or another.[3]

Sing or read through the *Kyrie Eleison.*[4] Offered here are three different musical settings of the ancient Greek text. Any of these short refrains can be sung meditatively in repetition or used frequently throughout the day as an "unceasing prayer" of repentance.

Basilea Schlink reminds us, "Just as it is true that we continually sin and continually need forgiveness, it is also true that repentance must continually pour into our hearts."[5]

This doesn't mean we must walk around in sackcloth and ashes, flagellating ourselves. It does mean, however, that we take our sin seriously, at times coming to the point of tears. For, as Schlink says, those who have wept over their sins "break out in rejoicing which is unknown to other hearts. The joy of forgiveness—no other joy can compare in depth and height!"[6]

In the liturgy, the *Kyrie* is followed by the *Gloria in Excelsis*—"Glory to God in the highest!" This is the song of rejoicing sung by the angels at the birth of Christ. Sing or speak the *Kyrie* again, and follow it with your own song of rejoicing. Praise God for the love, mercy, and forgiveness he has lavished upon us through his Son.

Questions of Examen and Exercises of Devotion

1. In what ways do I seek to justify myself before God and others?
2. Is there someone I have sinned against recently from whom I need to ask forgiveness?
3. Write or speak a prayer of confession, responding with the *Kyrie* after each petition. Conclude with a prayer of thanksgiving for the forgiving grace of God.
4. Read one of these penitential psalms (6, 32, 38, 51, 102, 130, 143) and use the *Kyrie* as a response after each phrase.

The Prayer of the Heart

Kyrie eleison. Lord, have mercy. Repentance is not a gift that I seek out. I don't like thinking about sin—especially mine. Help me, Lord, to receive the gift of repentance. Show me my sin, and give me a contrite heart. I thank you that in Jesus Christ I am forgiven—freely and forever. Amen.

Nothing but the Blood of Jesus

PLAINFIELD (7.8.7.8. with refrain)

Robert Lowry, 1876

Robert Lowry, 1876

1. What can wash a - way my sin? Noth-ing but the blood of Je - sus.
2. For my par - don this I see: noth-ing but the blood of Je - sus;
3. Noth - ing can for sin a - tone: noth-ing but the blood of Je - sus;
4. This is all my hope and peace: noth-ing but the blood of Je - sus;

What can make me whole a - gain? Noth-ing but the blood of Je - sus.
For my cleans-ing, this my plea: noth-ing but the blood of Je - sus.
Naught of good that I have done: noth-ing but the blood of Je - sus.
This is all my right - eous - ness: noth-ing but the blood of Je - sus.

Refrain

O! pre - cious is the flow that makes me white as snow;

No oth - er fount I know, noth - ing but the blood of Je - sus.

Scripture Reading: Hebrews 9

This passage focuses on Christ's priestly role and on the finality of his sacrifice for sin. See how the writer compares and contrasts the old and new covenants. The old covenant offered forgiveness on a limited scale and restricted access to an earthly sanctuary, the Holy of Holies. The new covenant offers complete, eternal forgiveness to all, and it provides free access through Christ, our high priest, into the heavenly sanctuary, into the very presence of God.

Scripture Meditation: Hebrews 9:12

. . . He entered once for all into the Holy Place, not with the blood of goats and calves, but with his own blood, thus obtaining eternal redemption.

Reflect on this verse. Center in on the phrase "with his own blood . . . eternal redemption." Hear the words of Jesus: "This cup that is poured out for you is the new covenant in my blood" (Luke 22:20). For you, personally. Ask God to help you grasp this shocking truth. Soak in this amazing reality. Thank him.

Reflecting in Song

Sing the first verse of the song. Notice the rhythmic repetition of the phrase "Nothing but the blood of Jesus," which is used twelve times in this song. This gospel song harks back to the camp-meeting days of the early 1800s. In camp meetings, the preacher would shout or sing a phrase, and the people would shout or sing a short, repetitive response. Read just the verses and hear the excitement of the camp meeting. In this call-and-response style even the early American frontier had its antiphonal singing.[7] These responses became known as choruses, and the camp-meeting choruses were often incorporated into the gospel hymns of the late nineteenth century.

Now, sing the song in its entirety. With its many repetitions and heavy emphasis on blood, it is sometimes said to be a gruesome song. But if it is, so are those parts of the Old Testament that detail the sacrifices. There is blood everywhere. God goes to great lengths to illustrate the point: sin is serious. "The person who sins shall die" (Ezek. 18:20). Blood must be shed, "for, as life, it is the blood that makes atonement" (Lev. 17:11). The New Testament confirms this same truth: "Without the shedding of blood there is no forgiveness of sins" (Heb. 9:22).

Some current theologies would discredit or discard the idea of blood. And it is tempting for us to make up our own theology—something easier to explain, more appealing, more saleable. The blood, like the cross, is offensive to modern sensibilities. But we do not believe something because of its outward appeal. We believe it because it is true. The Scriptures tell us, "You were ransomed . . . not with perishable things like silver or gold, but with the precious blood of Christ" (1 Peter 1:18–19). Besides, this is not only truth; this is love made visible.

"The true meaning of love is sacrifice," says writer Elisabeth Elliot.[8] The measure in which we are willing to sacrifice for another is the measure of our love. God loved so much that he gave the supreme sacrifice. In the shedding of his blood Christ loved us unto death. This is why we sing, over and over, "Nothing but the blood of Jesus!"

Questions of Examen and Exercises of Devotion

1. How is the blood of Christ "all my hope and peace"?
2. To what extent am I willing to sacrifice for a loved one? For an enemy?
3. In a group, try singing this song antiphonally, perhaps even shouting it back and forth, camp-meeting style.
4. Make a list of ways your life might be different without the reality this song celebrates.

The Prayer of the Heart

Dear Jesus, help me to realize more and more just what it means for you to have poured out your precious blood, your very life for me. Amen.

I Lay My Sins on Jesus

MUNICH (7.6.7.6.D.)
Meiningen *Gesangbuch*, 1613
Adapt. and harm. by Felix Mendelssohn, 1847

Horatius Bonar, 1843

Devotionally

1. I lay my sins on Je-sus, The spot-less Lamb of God;
2. I lay my wants on Je-sus; All full-ness dwells in him;
3. I rest my soul on Je-sus, This wear-y soul of mine,
4. I long to be like Je-sus, Meek, lov-ing, low-ly, mild;

He bears them all, and frees us From the ac-curs-ed load.
He heals all my dis-eas-es, He doth my soul re-deem.
His right hand me em-bra-ces; I on his breast re-cline.
I long to be, like Je-sus, The Fa-ther's ho-ly child.

I bring my guilt to Je-sus, To wash my crim-son stains
I lay my griefs on Je-sus, My bur-dens and my cares;
I love the name of Je-sus, Im-man-uel, Christ the Lord,
I long to be with Je-sus, A-mid the heaven-ly throng,

White in his Blood most pre-cious, Till not a spot re-mains.
He from them all re-leas-es, He all my sor-rows shares.
Like fra-grance on the breez-es His name a-broad is poured.
To sing with saints his prais-es, To learn the an-gels' song.

Scripture Reading: Isaiah 53:5–9, 1 Peter 2:21–25

As you read these passages, be aware of the parallels between them. Observe how Peter's words—"no deceit was found in his mouth," "by his wounds you have been healed," "you were going astray like sheep"—draw heavily upon the book of Isaiah. Notice how Peter points us to Christ as Suffering Servant and example, as Savior and healer, as Shepherd and guardian of our souls.

Scripture Meditation: 1 Peter 2:24

He himself bore our sins in his body on the cross,
so that, free from sins, we might live for righteousness;
by his wounds you have been healed.

Meditate on this Scripture. Affirm aloud as personal reality: "Lord, you yourself bore my sins in your body on the cross. . . ." Let these truths be absorbed into your heart: Christ died in my place, saving me from the guilt of sin, delivering me from the power of sin, healing me from the brokenness of sin.

Reflecting in Song

Sing or read through this hymn. It may be new to you, but it is an old hymn set to an even older melody. The words are by Horatius Bonar, a nineteenth-century Scottish hymn writer, and the tune is a seventeenth-century German chorale adapted and harmonized by Felix Mendelssohn.[9]

Horatius Bonar, a pastor, was Scotland's greatest hymnist. He was a man of contrasts—strong and powerful with a keen intellect, yet possessing a tender heart and a childlike faith. Many of his hymns were written for children because he felt that the psalmody being used in worship was too difficult for them to sing and understand.[10] This hymn, which he titled as both "The Substitute" and "The Fullness of Jesus," was written to teach children about the atonement. It was probably Bonar's first and certainly one of his finest hymns. It is typical of his work—simple, tender, intimate, yet profound and intensely spiritual.

Look at the first verse. Note how it reflects the Scripture passage, focusing on Christ as our sin bearer. As you sing it, lay your own sins on Jesus, releasing them and letting him take the load. Accept his forgiveness and cleansing.

Now, turn your attention to verse two. In some versions, the word *wants* has been changed to *needs*. While the change is understandable, it diminishes the scope of "the fullness of Jesus." Because we do not always know, we cannot fully separate our wants from our needs. But there is *nothing*, neither want nor need, that we cannot bring to him. The key is surrender. We lay our wants on Jesus and leave them there. He may fulfill them, he may change them, or he may give grace to live with them. With this understanding, sing the second verse and lay all of your wants, your hopes, your dreams, your needs, your burdens, your sorrows—all that you care about—on him. Take confidence in his sufficiency.

After giving him your sins, wants, and cares, you can rest in his love. Focus on verse three. Enter into the intimacy, the security, the comfort. Hear Jesus say, "Come . . . and I will give you rest" (Matt. 11:28). Sing this verse, all the while resting in the strength and protection of his everlasting arms.

Finally, look at verse four. Can you enter into its longing to be like Jesus and to be with Jesus? Lay these wants on him as you sing the last verse, knowing that these are wants he will surely satisfy.

Questions of Examen and Exercises of Devotion

1. Have I done some things this week that I should not have done?
2. Did I not do some things this week that I should have done?
3. Make a list of sins from this past week. Place the list in a can and light it, watching the paper turn to ashes as you sing this hymn.
4. Bonar wrote nearly six hundred hymns, many of which are still in use. All are wonderful devotional literature. Seek out one of them and use it in meditation.

The Prayer of the Heart

Lord Jesus, I lay my sins, my wants, my needs, my burdens, my worries on you. Sometimes I cannot tell them apart. But you can, and your grace is sufficient. I rest my heart and soul in you. Amen.

Jesus, Take Me as I Am

D. Bryant

D. Bryant

Tenderly

Je-sus, take me as I am.____ I can come no oth-er way.____

Take me deep-er in-to You.____ Make my flesh life melt a - way.____

Make me like a pre-cious stone,____ crys-tal clear and fine-ly honed;____

Life of Je-sus shin-ing through,____ Giv-ing glo-ry back to You.____

Accompaniment for this song is found on page 132.

Scripture Reading: Romans 12

In the first eleven chapters of Romans Paul sets forth the basic truths of the gospel: salvation by the grace of God, justification by faith in Christ, and sanctification by the Holy Spirit. In this chapter he begins to focus on the practical outworking of these truths. Observe how verses 1–2 form a transition for what follows. Notice the call to commitment of both body and mind.

Scripture Meditation: Romans 12:1

I appeal to you therefore, brothers and sisters, by the mercies of God, to present your bodies as a living sacrifice, holy and acceptable to God, which is your spiritual worship.

As you center on this verse, let it speak directly to you. Insert your name in place of *brothers and sisters*. Repeat the verse both silently and aloud. Now, read through the song, reflecting on ways it picks up themes from the Scripture text.

Reflecting in Song

A *living* sacrifice. Have you ever noticed how much easier it is to handle a dead sacrifice? Living sacrifices have a way of climbing off the altar, and they must be put back again and again and again. A living sacrifice takes a lifetime to be offered and involves the many little deaths of going beyond self.

The martyr's sacrifice is great indeed, but daily sacrifice—here is where our obedience is truly perfected. Yielding day by day, surrendering the most minute details, turning, always turning "till we come round right." Nothing will make the flesh life melt away—as our song says—like being a living sacrifice.

Ponder the first phrase of this song, "Jesus, take me as I am." Who I am, not who I want to be, is the only sacrifice I have to offer. I offer myself not on the basis of merit or deeds or virtue or earnest desire. I come "by the mercies of God." And by his mercy he takes me, receives me, welcomes me. "Just as I am, without one plea but that thy blood was shed for me."

God takes us as we are, and he loves us as we are. But he loves us too much to leave us as we are. "Heartily He loves you, heartily He hates the evil in you—so heartily that He will even cast you into the fire to burn you clean," says George MacDonald.[11] Job, in the midst of suffering, affirmed that "when he has tested me, I shall come out like gold" (Job 23:10). God wants to make each of us into something pure and beautiful, something priceless and enduring.

Sing the entire song, giving special attention to the words "Make me like a precious stone, crystal clear and finely honed."

A diamond is the most precious of stones. It is made out of carbon, a common substance that is the basic chemical component of all living things. Carbon can be soft, black, and opaque, such as in graphite. But if subjected to intense pressure and heat over a long period of time, carbon can become a diamond—the clearest, purest, and hardest of all natural substances. It is so hard that it can be cut and polished only with another diamond.

God "does not willingly afflict or grieve anyone" (Lam. 3:33) but he uses the pressures, the trials, and the suffering in our lives to make us into precious stones. He allows us to be perfectly cut and polished so that we might attain our greatest possible brilliance.

The essence of a diamond's beauty is reflection. It has no light of its own but only reflects the source of light. The more perfectly it reflects, the more lovely it becomes. The light of Jesus is our beauty, "and all of us . . . seeing the glory of the Lord as though reflected in a mirror, are being transformed into the same image from one degree of glory to another" (2 Cor. 3:18).

Now, sing the song once more. Let it be your prayer as you offer yourself to God yet again as a living sacrifice.

Questions of Examen and Exercises of Devotion

1. When have I tried to come to God in ways other than just as I am, for example, via my own cleverness or supposed superiority?
2. Are there areas of my life that I honestly cannot offer to God at this time?
3. Sing this song several times a day for a few days as a prayer of offering yourself to God.
4. What aspects of Romans 12 would I like to see incorporated more fully into my life? What actions can I take this next month to begin the process?

The Prayer of the Heart

Jesus, take me as I am. I can come no other way. Take me deeper into you. Make my flesh life melt away. Make me like a precious stone, crystal clear and finely honed, life of Jesus shining through, giving glory back to you. Amen.

Holy Ground

Christopher Beatty

Christopher Beatty

This is (1.2.) ho - ly ground, we're stand-ing on ho - ly ground,
(3.4.) ho - ly hands, He's giv-en us ho - ly hands,

for the Lord is here and where He is is
He works through these hands and so these hands are

ho - ly.
ho - ly.

2. This is
4. These are

for the
He works

Lord is here, and where He is is ho - ly.
through these hands, and so these hands are ho - ly.

Fine

D.S. al Fine

3. These are

Scripture Reading: Exodus 3:1–15, 4:1–17

This passage, which includes the first use of the word *holy* in the Bible, provides humanity's initial glimpse into the holiness of God. Even the ground surrounding God's manifest presence is holy. Observe Moses' reaction. A mere glimpse of this holiness is too much for human eyes. See how God takes Moses as he is and uses what he has—common, everyday things: his shepherd's staff, his hands, his mouth.

Scripture Meditation: Exodus 3:5

Remove the sandals from your feet, for the place on which you are standing is holy ground.

As you dwell on this Scripture passage, see if you can identify with Moses. Experience along with him your first hint of the holiness of God. Witness the overwhelming majesty and splendor, the perfection and purity. Know that you are on holy ground. Sing the song, and worship God in his holiness.

Reflecting in Song

"This is holy ground." We tend to think of holy ground as being at some other place or time—a beautiful cathedral, maybe, or a specially anointed time of worship. "Holy hands"—the hands of a bishop, a pastor, a missionary, perhaps? Yes, but holiness is also here and now for each of us. The incarnation has brought holiness into everyday life: Emmanuel—God with us. The veil of the temple separating the holy from the common has been removed. Though we are still sinners, God sees us as his holy ones, saints, because of the blood of Jesus. And all created things, including the common and the ordinary, share in the reconciliation (Col. 1:20).

Our human tendency is to divide and classify, making distinctions between sacred and secular worlds, spiritual and material pursuits, holy and common things. We consider certain work to be "Christian work." We separate and segregate, and by doing so we avoid giving God total control of our lives. True holiness, however, consists in an integrated life—a life lived "wholly unto God."[12] All good, honest work offered to Christ is full-time Christian work, holy work. The hands that do it are holy hands.

Moses, shepherding on a lonely mountain, was a witness to the holiness of God and the first to know God's name. Similarly, shepherds in a field near Bethle-hem saw the glory of God and were the first (other than Mary and Joseph) to see God in the flesh. Moses was called out by God to a special task, to be the deliverer of Israel. The shepherds of Bethlehem, remaining nameless, returned to their sheep. Yet their common, ordinary work was holy, too, for they went "glorifying and praising God" (Luke 2:20). Martin Luther comments regarding these shepherds, "Next to faith this is the highest art—to be content with the calling in which God has placed you. I have not learned it yet."[13]

May we like the shepherds learn that art. May we live lives of holy obedience in all of the tasks to which God has called us. May we see them—the mundane as well as the spectacular—as holy work.

Now, sing the song again. Offer your hands, your work, your life as holy, and wholly unto God.

Questions of Examen and Exercises of Devotion

1. Are there areas of my life that I have separated from the "spiritual," thereby denying God control of them?
2. What are the tasks to which God has called me? Am I content in them?
3. God had to tell Moses to take off his shoes; he did not know it was holy ground. Can you see the place where you live and work as holy ground?
4. For the next few days be especially attentive to the sacred in the most trivial of things.

The Prayer of the Heart

O Lord, Holy God, thank you for entering into this world and sanctifying it by your very presence. No task was too common, too earthly, for you. I look to your example as you sawed boards, hammered nails, washed feet. May I be content in my calling, knowing that I am serving on holy ground. Amen.

Hide Me in Your Holiness

Steve Ragsdale

Steve Ragsdale

Hide me, Lord, in Your ho - li - ness, ev - 'ry

sin I now con - fess. Praise to You for-

giv - ing Lord, hide me in Your ho - li - ness,

hide me in Your ho - li - ness.

Scripture Reading: Colossians 2:1–3:4

Throughout Colossians Paul stresses the supremacy and complete sufficiency of Christ. He uses words like *all, every, whole, fullness.* Give attention to this emphasis as you read the Scripture passage.

Scripture Meditation: Colossians 3:2–3

Set your minds on things that are above, not on things that are on earth, for you have died, and your life is hidden with Christ in God.

As you meditate on this text, let your thoughts turn to things above—things of God. Think on the holiness, the wholeness, the sufficiency of Christ "in whom the whole fullness of deity dwells bodily" (v. 9). Speak affirmations of his holiness. Realize that you are "hidden with Christ in God." You are very near to God's heart. Sing the song. Let your singing of the song draw you into the divine center.

Reflecting in Song

This song reminds us that the holiness of Christ is ours. God has made him to be our "righteousness and sanctification and redemption" (1 Cor. 1:30). No, we are not yet perfect in all our practice. We are "at the same time saints and sinners."[14] We are constantly growing into the holiness God has already given. As with much of the working of God, this is a great paradox and mystery. But it is true. Joyfully claim the holiness that is yours in Christ as you sing this song once more.

Sometimes the word *holiness* conjures up negative images: rigid rules, stringent self-denial, preoccupation with sin. Yes, obedience, self-denial, and repentance are all aspects of holiness, but they can be overemphasized. When holiness gets out of balance, it becomes distorted and restrictive, legalistic and self-centered.

Holiness is not negative; it is positive. It is not confining; it is liberating. Holiness is wholeness. It is all that Christ is: purity and beauty, grace and truth, goodness and love. And because he "is all and in all" (Col. 3:11), we see signs of his holiness all around. George MacDonald, reflecting on the delicate beauty of frost and snow one winter day, marveled at "the principle which, in the wildest, most lawless, fantastically chaotic, apparently capricious work of nature, always kept it beautiful. The beauty of holiness must be at the heart of it somehow, I thought. Because our God is so free

from stain, so loving, so unselfish, so good, so altogether what He wants us to be, so holy, therefore all His works declare Him in beauty."[15] Whatever is beautiful, whatever is true, whatever is good—all speak forth the holiness of Christ. Sing the song, reflecting on the "beauty of holiness."

In God's holiness, in his perfection, is also protection. The holiness of Christ is our surest defense against the sin and evil that are within and around us. "Thou art my hiding place and my shield" (Ps. 119:114). In God is everything good, everything we need.

Sing this song once more. Know the sufficiency of Christ. Show forth the beauty of Christ. Grow into the likeness of Christ, into the holiness that is yours in him.

Questions of Examen and Exercises of Devotion

1. In what way has Christ proven himself sufficient for me?
2. What signs of the "beauty of holiness" do I see around me today?
3. Pray the phrase "Hide me in your holiness" often throughout the day as an unceasing prayer.
4. In every activity of this next week picture yourself hidden in the holiness of God.

The Prayer of the Heart

When my sin overwhelms me:
　　Hide me, Lord, in your holiness.

When I act unholy, unlovely:
　　Hide me, Lord, in your holiness.

When the desires of my heart are not yours:
　　Hide me, Lord, in your holiness.

When I feel defiled by sins not my own:
　　Hide me, Lord, in your holiness.

When the evil all around seems to be closing in:
　　Hide me, Lord, in your holiness.

Because I have no holiness, no righteousness, no goodness of my own, but only by the power of your precious blood:
　　Hide me, Lord, in your holiness. Amen.

Change My Heart, O God

Eddie Espinosa   Eddie Espinosa

Scripture Reading: Psalm 51

Psalm 51 is David's cry for mercy, his own *Kyrie eleison,* upon conviction of his sin—murdering Uriah the Hittite and taking Uriah's wife for himself. As you read this model prayer of contrition, note David's expressions of sorrow, confession, repentance, forgiveness, cleansing, restoration, witness, worship, renewal. See how passionate the psalm is and how David takes personal responsibility for his sin: *my* transgressions, *my* iniquity.

Scripture Meditation: Psalm 51:10

Create in me a clean heart, O God,
and put a new and right spirit within me.

Focus on this verse and fix it in your memory. Contemplate it, and consider what it is requesting: a clean heart; a new and right (steadfast) spirit. Examine your heart with regard to it. Now, sing the song quietly.

Reflecting in Song

Notice in this psalm—this prayer of David's heart—the unashamed emotional display of grief over sin. This is "godly grief," the grief that produces repentance (2 Cor. 7:10). It leads to action: actual turning from sin. Such grief is uncommon today. Sin, if it is acknowledged at all, is usually taken lightly with an attitude of "do it now; you can apologize later" or "God will forgive—that's his job." Or sin is excused as a consequence of heredity or environment. Or it is said to be the result of "low self-esteem."

Sin is not a result of low self-esteem; it is a cause of it. The fact is that I am a sinner and I do fall short of the glory of God, and no amount of positive input or self-affirmation will change this fact if I fail to accept the affirming love and forgiveness of God.

Placing responsibility elsewhere does not remove sin. So often we excuse ourselves with "that's the way I was raised" (blaming others) or "that's the way I was made" (blaming God). These are contributing factors, to be sure, and often we have deep wounds from them that need healing. But these factors are not an excuse for sin. We are not helpless, hopeless victims. In life's situations we *can* choose the good, the true, the beautiful because "God is faithful, and . . . with the temptation will also provide the way of escape" (1 Cor. 10:13, RSV). To deny the reality of sin or to fail to take it seriously and personally bars us from experiencing the mercy, grace, and love of God in all its fullness. As a result, we fail to know the joy of God's salvation.

Thomas More knew the grace and love of God in his "sweet Saviour Christ," and he took his sin seriously. In 1535, just days before his scheduled execution by Henry VIII, he wrote "A Devout Prayer."[16] It is a profound expression of sorrow for sin, a plea for holiness and for "grace to amend my life." More concludes his prayer with a portion from the *Te Deum,* "Deign, O Lord, to keep us on that day without sin."

What would be my last wish if I knew I had but a few days to live? Would it be for holiness and purity? Would it be, "Create in me a clean heart, O God"?

Open your heart to God's loving Spirit and ask him to reveal your sin, your need of cleansing. Give him time. Such a revelation is a lifelong process—something we cannot bear to see all at once. Receive what God shows you today. Ask him to give you a longing for purity, a passion for a clean heart. Prayerfully sing the song and offer your heart to him.

Questions of Examen and Exercises of Devotion

1. Do I truly desire for my heart to be changed? What aspects of change make me uncomfortable?
2. Am I willing to submit to that which brings cleansing?
3. Pray meditatively through Psalm 51, singing the first half of this song (eight bars) as a response after each verse.
4. Choose a characteristic attitude that you feel could be more pleasing to God and then see what you can do this next week to strengthen the corresponding virtue (for example, moving from cowardice to courage, criticism to charity, stinginess to generosity).

The Prayer of the Heart

O God, give me a burning desire for your holiness and your wholeness. Show my sin for what it is. Work your cleansing. May I settle for nothing less than a heart made pure and clean and beautiful. Amen.

May the Mind of Christ My Savior

ST. LEONARDS (8.7.8.5.)

Kate B. Wilkinson, 1925

A. Cyril Barham-Gould, 1925

1. May the mind of Christ my Sav-ior live in me from day to day,
2. May the Word of God dwell rich-ly in my heart from hour to hour,
3. May the peace of God my Fa-ther rule my life in ev-ery-thing,
4. May the love of Je - sus fill me as the wa - ters fill the sea,
5. May I run the race be - fore me, strong and brave to face the foe,

By his love and power con-trol-ling all I do and say.
So that all may see I tri-umph on - ly through his power.
That I may be calm to com-fort sick and sor - row - ing.
Him ex - alt - ing, self a - bas - ing— this is vic - to - ry.
Look-ing on - ly un - to Je - sus as I on - ward go.

Scripture Reading: Philippians 2:1–11

The book of Philippians has been called a "Christian love letter," so great was Paul's love, devotion, and gratitude to the church at Philippi. Follow as Paul begins this passage with a plea for unity among the believers, then tells them how to achieve it: by having the mind of Christ. The key to unity lies in humility modeled in Christ himself.

Scripture Meditation: Philippians 2:5–7

Let the same mind be in you that was in Christ Jesus, who, though he was in the form of God, did not regard equality with God as something to be exploited, but emptied himself, taking the form of a slave, being born in human likeness.

As you ponder these verses, think on what Christ gave up in becoming human: wealth, rank, title, prestige, honor, glory, power. Consider how obtaining these very things has driven humanity throughout history. See what Christ did with them. Let the Holy Spirit search your heart and reveal to you ways in which any of these are driving you. Ask God to give you the mind of Christ.

Reflecting in Song

Sing through this hymn, entering into its attitude of "spiritual receptivity."[17] Pause after each verse and ask the Spirit to help you receive as the verse specifies: the mind of Christ; the Word of God; the peace of God; the love of Jesus. In singing verse five, call to mind Hebrews 12:1, "Let us run with perseverance the race that is set before us, looking to Jesus." Pray that you might do this.

Give attention to verse four: "him exalting, self abasing." To abase means, literally, "to lower." We lower ourselves, taking on the humility of Christ who "emptied himself." We seek the lowest place, do the lowest thing, and die to the need to be recognized.

Humility is often confused with degrading or demeaning ourselves. In *The Screwtape Letters,* C. S. Lewis has Screwtape, that high-level tempter, say, "You must . . . conceal from the patient the true end of Humility. Let him think of it, not as self-forgetfulness, but as a certain kind of opinion (namely, a low opinion) of his own talents and character."[18] As Lewis reminds us, humility is not in demeaning ourselves. True humility is

in forgetting ourselves. George MacDonald calls this self-forgetfulness "the healthiest of mental conditions. One has to look to his *way,* to his *deeds,* to his *conduct—* not to himself."[19] Sing the fourth verse again and think of "self abasing" as "self forgetting."

In the mind of Christ, the humility of Christ, says Paul, is the harmony of the body of Christ. Just imagine a church where everyone instead of vying for prestigious roles is scrambling to tend the nursery, polish the floor, clean the toilets. Imagine a church where no one cares who gets the credit, the dollars, or the members as long God is glorified. Imagine a church where no one argues over music!

Can I do my part to promote harmony within the body of Christ? Can I follow the example of Christ and forsake a high-visibility role in favor of an invisible one? Can I rejoice when someone else's gifts are used and esteemed above mine? Can I enjoy the favorite music of others even if it is not mine simply because of the pleasure it brings to them? I can if I have the mind of Christ. Sing and pray this song again. Sing, "May the mind of Christ my Savior live in me *this very day.*"

Questions of Examen and Exercises of Devotion

1. Is there an invisible task to which Christ is calling me today? Can I do it in a spirit of self-forgetfulness?
2. Is there a highly visible task to which Christ is calling me today? Can I do it in a spirit of self-forgetfulness?
3. Think of someone who has gifts, talents, or a ministry similar to your own, someone with whom you perhaps feel in competition. Pray that God will prosper his or her work.
4. By changing the personal pronouns to *your* or *our* this song can become a benediction, a group prayer, a blessing. Try praying it in any of these ways.

The Prayer of the Heart

Lord Jesus, may your mind live in me today. Amen.

Trust and Obey

TRUST AND OBEY (6.6.9.D. with refrain)

John H. Sammis, 1887

Daniel B. Towner, 1887

1. When we walk with the Lord in the light of his Word, what a glo-ry he
2. Not a bur-den we bear, not a sor-row we share, but our toil he will
3. But we nev-er can prove the de-lights of his love un-til all on the
4. Then in fel-low-ship sweet we will sit at his feet, or we'll walk by his

sheds on our way! While we do his good will, he a-bides with us
rich-ly re-pay; Not a grief nor a loss, not a frown nor a
al-tar we lay; For the fa-vor he shows and the joy he be-
side in the way; What he says we will do, where he sends we will

Refrain

still, and with all who will trust and o-bey. Trust and o-bey, for there's
cross, but is blest if we trust and o-bey.
stows are for them who will trust and o-bey.
go— nev-er fear, on-ly trust and o-bey.

no oth-er way to be hap-py in Je-sus, but to trust and o-bey.

Scripture Reading: James 2:14–26

The book of James is primarily a book of practical obedience. James speaks to believers, calling them to continual discipleship and urging them to "be doers of the word" (1:22). As you read this portion, be aware of the interdependence of faith and works.

Scripture Meditation: James 2:26

For just as the body without the spirit is dead,
so faith without works is also dead.

Repeat this verse until you can say it by heart. Reflect on the analogy of body and spirit, faith and works. The word *spirit* is closely associated with breath: as the spirit is breath to our bodies, so works are breath to our faith. Recall the first time you found this to be true—your works, your acts of obedience giving life to your faith. Now, sing the refrain, "Trust and obey."

Reflecting in Song

This gospel song was born out of a revival meeting held by D. L. Moody in Brockton, Massachusetts, in the late 1800s. When the invitation was given, a young man spoke out in response, "I am not quite sure—but I am going to trust, and I am going to obey." These words struck the music leader, Daniel Towner, who jotted them down and sent them to his friend, the Reverend J. H. Sammis. Rev. Sammis wrote this hymn, which Towner then set to music.[20]

As you sing this hymn, think of that young man and of the far-reaching influence of his obedience in the face of doubt.

Trust and obey; faith and obedience. So often we try to separate them or argue over which is more important, which should come first. But George MacDonald reminds us that "what in the heart we call faith, in the will we call obedience."[21] Faith and obedience are an inseparable unity, a symbiotic relationship with each depending upon the other, each giving life to the other. Faith manifests in obedience, and obedience begets faith. They are of the same essence, and it is impossible to know which comes first. Nor do we need to. "Obey the truth," says MacDonald, "and let theory wait. Theory may spring from life, but never life from theory."[22]

Sometimes we think, "Oh, if only I had enough faith, I would . . ." We want to wait until we have sufficient faith built up to do some great work. But that moment will never come. It is not a matter of having enough faith and then doing something spectacular. It is a matter of stepping out in obedience in the small thing, the thing close at hand, despite wavering faith. And these small steps of obedience will exercise our faith, breathing life into it and making it grow stronger. Sing the song again, especially noticing the refrain and how one little word makes all the difference. It is not "trust *or* obey" or "trust, *then* obey." It is "trust *and* obey."

Questions of Examen and Exercises of Devotion

1. How do I experience my faith influencing my actions? How do I experience my actions, my obedience, influencing my faith?
2. Is there an area in which I find obedience to be especially difficult? In what small way might I take a step into obedience?
3. Consider verse four: "What he says we will do, where he sends we will go." Examine your commitments in light of these words. Are any changes in order?
4. List three actions you can do this next week that will give expression to and deepen your faith.

The Prayer of the Heart

O Lord, my Lord, trust seems far away, doubt near at hand. Give me the will to obey, even—especially—in the face of my doubt. Show me the thing you would have me do yet today. Amen.

Songs of the Spirit

Wonderful, wonderful in the sight of angels, a great wonder in the
eyes of faith, to see the giver of being, the generous sustainer and ruler
of everything that is, in the manger in swaddling clothes and with nowhere
to lay his head, and yet the bright host of glory worshipping him now.

Thanks forever, and a hundred thousand thanks, thanks while there is
breath in me, that there is an object to worship and a theme for a song to
last forever . . . a babe, weak, powerless, the infinite true and loving God.

—*Ann Griffiths*

For those who follow Christ, all of our singing and all of our living can
be one huge *Jubilate Deo*. Jubilant in song and jubilant in life, we proclaim
Christ's resurrection until he returns. And even more, the very same
Spirit that raised Jesus from the dead dwells in us, animating our lives
(Rom. 8:11).

Music is certainly a medium appropriate for this wonderful message.
Singing and dancing, shouting and celebrating, we bear witness to a per-
petual jubilee of the Spirit. The Spirit who empowers us also inspires in us
the joy of ecstatic celebration. A continual *Te Deum* arises from our hearts.

Joy—deep, rich, full joy—is the mark of life in the Spirit. St. Augustine
declares, "The Christian should be an alleluia from head to foot!" And
God, through the prophet Isaiah, reminds us:

> *Be glad and rejoice for ever*
> *in that which I create;*
> *for behold, I create Jerusalem a rejoicing,*
> *and her people a joy.* (RSV)

So, it is not just the trees of the fields that clap their hands; we do as well.

How Majestic Is Your Name

Michael W. Smith

Michael W. Smith

O Lord, our Lord, how ma - jes - tic is your name in all the
earth. O earth. O Lord, we praise your name. O Lord,
we mag - ni - fy your name: Prince of Peace, Might - y God, O
Lord God Al - might - y. O y.

Scripture Reading:
2 Chronicles 20:1–23, Psalm 8:1–2

As you read the Chronicles passage, observe how King Jehoshaphat and the people of Judah responded when surrounded by their enemies. First, they fasted and prayed. Then, everyone—even the children—listened to the Spirit of the Lord. And finally, they obeyed. And what ushered in victory? "As they began to sing and praise, the Lord sent an ambush" (v. 22). Read Psalm 8:1–2 in light of this story.

Scripture Meditation: Psalm 8:1 (NIV)

Begin your meditation by asking God's Spirit to touch your spirit, to set you free to worship him. Wait in quietness, and open your heart to his touch. Repeat the Scripture verse and enter into praise:

> O Lord, our Lord, how majestic is your name in all the earth!

Sing the song worshipfully. Let your soul ascend in "self-forgetting adoration"[1] and witness the majesty and power of God. Continue to minister to the Lord with words of praise and thanksgiving, love and adoration.

Reflecting in Song

To worship God, to give praise and adoration to the Lord of creation, is our main work in life. The Westminster Catechism reminds us, "Man's chief end is to glorify God, and to enjoy Him forever."[2]

So often we give God in praise and worship the leftovers of our lives. Yes, we may set aside an hour on Sunday. But for the most part worship and praise wait until we feel like it or until we can get around to it. We let urgent tasks draw us away from this most important task, feeling the pressing need to accomplish something tangible or "productive." Perhaps we have a defective view of worship.

Worship is powerful. As we see in the Scripture, praising God puts armies to flight. The armies standing against us, unlike those against Judah, are of the invisible variety, but they are no less real. They are, in fact, more real, more formidable. They are the "spiritual forces of evil in the heavenly places" (Eph. 6:12). For these battles our only help is in "the name of the Lord, who made heaven and earth" (Ps. 124:8). Sing the song and picture your enemy being put to flight.

Worship is productive. It is meaningful work. Under David's leadership it became a full-time job for some of the priests "to invoke, to thank and to praise the LORD" (1 Chron. 16:4). You and I are now part of that priesthood, the priesthood of all believers. The ministry of worship has become our vocation, our calling, as well. Sing the song again. Realize that this may be the most important work you do today.

Worship is creative, fulfilling work. In worship, our spirits touch the Spirit of the Creator of the universe! It brings incomparable fulfillment and joy. And we "enjoy Him forever." Our praises join with those of saints throughout the ages and those of the great angelic host, and they will ring throughout eternity. Worship is enduring, eternal work.

Yet, even these are not the main reasons we worship God. We worship him because he is worthy. That is what worship is—declaring God's "worth-ship." And our worship brings joy to his heart. Just as the words "Daddy, I love you! You're the most wonderful dad in the world!" bring joy to a father's heart, so God is blessed by our words of love and adoration.

All of creation knows and proclaims God's praise. Ambrose says, "Anyone (who has) his five wits should blush with shame if he did not begin the day with a psalm, since even the tiniest birds open and close the day with sweet songs of devotion."[3] Shall we do anything less?

Questions of Examen and Exercises of Devotion

1. What kind of priority do I give to worship?
2. When have I known the praises of God to put an enemy to flight?
3. During the coming week, let the song of the birds be your personal call to worship. Pause, repeat the Scripture verse, and sing this or some other song of praise.
4. Give God the firstfruits of your day. This next week schedule some specific times on your calendar when you will minister to him in praise and worship.

The Prayer of the Heart

O Lord, our Lord, how majestic is your name in all the earth! (Gently speak or sing these words several times, allowing a spirit of worship to come in whatever way pleases God; silent adoration or jubilant celebration.)

Holy God, We Praise Thy Name

German, XVIII century, Tr. Clarence A. Walworth, 1853
Based on *Te Deum Laudamus*, 4th cent. Latin

GROSSER GOTT, WIR LOBEN DICH (7.8.7.8.7.7.)
Allgemeines Katholisches Gesangbuch, Vienna, 1774

1. Ho - ly God, we praise Thy name; Lord of all, we bow be - fore Thee;
2. Hark, the loud ce - les - tial hymn, An - gel choirs a - bove are rais - ing;
3. Lo! The ap - os - tol - ic train Join Thy sa - cred name to hal - low;
4. Ho - ly Fa - ther, Ho - ly Son, Ho - ly Spir - it, Three we name Thee;

All on earth Thy scep - ter claim, All in heav'n a - bove a - dore Thee.
Cher - u - bim and Ser - a - phim, In un - ceas - ing cho - rus prais - ing,
Pro - phets swell the glad re - frain, And the white - robed mar - tyrs fol - low;
While in es - sence on - ly One, Un - di - vid - ed God we claim Thee,

In - fi - nite Thy vast do - main, Ev - er - last - ing is Thy reign.
Fill the heav'ns with sweet ac - cord: Ho - ly, ho - ly, ho - ly Lord.
And, from morn to set of sun, Through the Church the song goes on.
And a - dor - ing bend the knee, While we own the mys - ter - y.

"Holy God, We Praise Thy Name" is based on an early Latin hymn, the *Te Deum Laudamus*. Considered one of the finest hymns of Christendom, the *Te Deum* combines adoration and praise with a confession of faith and a prayer for help. It is offered here in its entirety for reading and meditation. As you read, notice the focus of each section. Follow the progression from beginning to end as it moves from a magnificent expression of corporate worship to an intensely personal plea for mercy.

We praise Thee, O God: we acknowledge Thee to be the Lord.
All the earth doth worship Thee, the Father everlasting.
To Thee all angels cry aloud, the Heavens and all the powers therein.
To Thee Cherubim and Seraphim continually do cry:
Holy, Holy, Holy, Lord God of Sabaoth;
Heaven and earth are full of the majesty of Thy glory.
The glorious company of the Apostles praise Thee.
The goodly fellowship of the Prophets praise Thee.
The noble army of Martyrs praise Thee.
The holy Church throughout all the world doth acknowledge Thee;
The Father of an infinite Majesty;
Thine honourable, true, and only Son;
Also the Holy Ghost, the Comforter.

Thou art the King of Glory, O Christ.
Thou art the everlasting Son of the Father.
When Thou tookest upon Thee to deliver man,
Thou didst not abhor the Virgin's womb.
When Thou hadst overcome the sharpness of death,
Thou didst open the Kingdom of Heaven to all believers.
Thou sittest at the right hand of God in the glory of the Father.
We believe that Thou shalt come to be our Judge.
We therefore pray Thee, help Thy servants
Whom Thou hast redeemed with Thy precious blood.
Make them to be numbered with Thy Saints in glory everlasting.

O Lord, save Thy people and bless Thine heritage.
Govern them, and lift them up forever.
Day by day we magnify Thee;
And we worship Thy name, ever world without end.
Vouchsafe, O Lord, to keep us this day without sin.
O Lord, have mercy upon us: have mercy upon us.

O Lord, let Thy mercy lighten upon us, as our trust is in Thee.
O Lord, in Thee have I trusted: Let me never be confounded.

Tradition attributes the *Te Deum* to Ambrose and Augustine, who were said to have composed it spontaneously upon the occasion of Augustine's baptism on Easter, A.D. 387. Whether this is true or not, we do know that the *Te Deum* dates back to the fourth century and has been one of the most widely sung hymns of the Church ever since. It has been sung in many languages and paraphrases using many different tunes and musical forms—everything from simple chants to grand choral works. It has been sung in recognition of special festivals and in celebration of great events. It has been sung by pilgrims fleeing persecution and by martyrs facing death.

The hymn "Holy God, We Praise Thy Name" is an English translation of the popular German *Te Deum*, "Grosser Gott, wir loben Dich," which dates back to an eighteenth-century Roman Catholic hymnal. These four verses paraphrase the first section of the *Te Deum*. Read the hymn and compare it with the *Te Deum*. Give attention to the strong affirmation of the Trinity in verse four of the hymn. Now, sing it in quiet adoration. Know that you are joining with believers throughout history. You are part of an unending song of praise to God.

Questions of Examen and Exercises of Devotion

1. Are there ways the *Te Deum* challenges and corrects my own beliefs?
2. 1 Chronicles 29:10–13 is David's personal *Te Deum Laudamus*. Use it in praise and meditation. Consider writing out your own *Te Deum*.
3. In liturgical traditions the *Te Deum* has been a part of matins, or morning prayer, for centuries. Begin your day in worship by reading the *Te Deum* or by singing "Holy God, We Praise Thy Name."
4. Some of the better-known settings of the *Te Deum* are by composers G. F. Handel, Anton Bruckner, Benjamin Britten, and John Rutter. Check out or buy a recording of one of them. Listen. Enjoy. Worship.

The Prayer of the Heart

Holy God, Almighty Lord, all praise and honor be to you. Thank you that through Jesus Christ I can join the eternal song of apostles and prophets, saints and angels. To you alone be glory for ever and ever! Amen.

Jubilate Deo
(Rejoice in God)
(Six-part canon)

From Psalm 100   Praetorius

Ju - bi - la - te De - o, Ju - bi - la - te De - o, Al - le - lu - ia.

Rejoice, Give Thanks and Sing

Edward H. Plumptre, 1865   Arthur H. Messiter, 1883

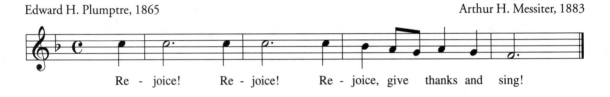

Re - joice! Re - joice! Re - joice, give thanks and sing!

Come Into His Presence
(Four-part round)

From Psalm 100   Source unknown

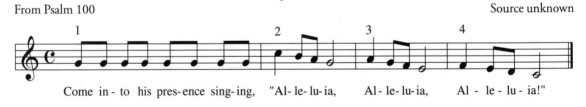

Come in - to his pres-ence sing-ing, "Al- le-lu-ia, Al- le-lu-ia, Al - le - lu - ia!"

Scripture Reading: Psalm 100

This psalm is sometimes known as the "*Jubilate*," so named for its opening Latin phrase, "*Jubilate Deo*"[4] ("Rejoice in God"). As you read the psalm, pay attention to all of the commands in the first four verses. Then notice the reason for them as given in verse five.

Scripture Meditation: Psalm 100:1–2

Make a joyful noise to the Lord, all the earth.
Worship the Lord with gladness;
Come into his presence with singing.

Do as the psalm says! It is not referring to some other time or place; it means here and now. Rejoice in God. Make a joyful noise. Lift up your hands and your heart in worship. Enter his presence with a song of praise. Use one of the three songs here or any other song of rejoicing.

Reflecting in Song

These three short, simple songs all echo Psalm 100. The first, "*Jubilate Deo*," is a six-part canon or round written by the sixteenth-century German composer Michael Praetorius. The second, "Rejoice," is actually the refrain of a nineteenth-century hymn,[5] and "Come into His Presence" is a contemporary, four-part round. Sing through each of them.

Throughout Scripture and especially in the psalms we are told, "Sing to the Lord!" Singing is not considered optional. God expects, even commands us to sing. And we know that "his commandments are not burdensome" (1 John 5:3). Martin Luther reminds us, "God does not demand great sacrifices or precious treasures of great price for His blessings. No, He asks for the easiest work of all, namely to sing and praise."[6]

Maybe you are saying, "But *I* can't sing!" Is that really true? Some people do have physical conditions that prevent singing, but more often people have been told early in life by parents, teachers, or friends that they cannot sing. And, tragically, the message has been believed. Perhaps you have been pointed at, laughed at, or singled out in some way for the way you sing. Our society promotes the idea that either you are a born singer or else you can't sing. A proliferation of electronically enhanced, recorded music makes us think we can never sound as good, and as a result we refuse to try. Often slick, recorded lullabies put infants to sleep instead of a mother's or father's imperfect voice. No wonder so many of us grow up thinking that we can't sing.

Perhaps you do not read music, sing in tune, or have a great sense of rhythm. That does not matter to God. Just as "the Lord does not see as mortals see" but "looks on the heart" (1 Sam. 16:7), so he does not hear as we hear. He hears the song of our hearts. He blesses it and uses it to bless others. More people are moved to tears by a sincere, heartfelt expression of song with all its imperfections than by a polished, professional performance that lacks heart. This is not to say the two are mutually exclusive or that God does not want us to practice. When the song of the heart combines with the gift of talent and the discipline of practice, it brings a special blessing. But too often we think that if we do not have the talent or the training, then we should not sing at all.

Singing is an essential discipline of the Christian life, and it can be learned and practiced. And it is never too late. Ask the Holy Spirit to put his song in your heart. Invite him to heal any insecurities, any hurts from the past. Step out in faith, open your mouth, and sing. Let your song be your offering. Sing from your heart, and know that God smiles with pleasure. Make a joyful noise to the Lord! *Jubilate Deo!*

Questions of Examen and Exercises of Devotion

1. How do I carry out the commands of Psalm 100:1–4? How might I do better?
2. In what ways have I experienced the goodness, steadfast love, and faithfulness of God (v. 5)?
3. Read Psalm 100. Respond by singing one of these three songs after each verse.
4. Take a walk and hear the songs of "*Jubilate*" in the birds of the air and all creatures of the earth. Join in with your own song of rejoicing.

The Prayer of the Heart

O Lord, I do rejoice in you. I do worship you. Fill my heart with song. And may the song of my heart be sweet music to you. Amen.

In the Presence of Your People

(The Celebration Song)

Psalm 22:3, 22; 145:7; para. Brent Chambers, 1977

CELEBRATION (Irregular)
Brent Chambers, 1977

In the pres-ence of your peo-ple I will praise your name,

For a - lone you are ho - ly, en - throned on the prais - es of Is - ra - el.

Let us cel - e - brate your good - ness and your stead - fast love;

May your name be ex - alt - ed here on earth and in heaven a - bove.

Scripture Reading:
Psalm 149:1–4, Ephesians 5:18–20

The summons to corporate worship is found in both the Old and New Testaments as shown in these two Scripture passages. In reading, notice that worship is a physical and emotional activity as well as a spiritual one. Appreciate the varied expressions of the arts: instrumental music, song, dance.

Scripture Meditation: Ephesians 5:18b–19

Be filled with the Spirit, as you sing psalms and hymns and spiritual songs among yourselves, singing and making melody to the Lord in your hearts.

Singing is a joyful response to being filled with the Spirit, and, according to St. Chrysostom, it is also a means of being filled, for "the words [of spiritual songs] purify the mind, and the Holy Spirit descends swiftly upon the mind of the singer."[7] The Spirit begets song, and spiritual songs invoke the Spirit. Now, reflect on this Scripture. Consider it personally as well as in the wider context of the body of Christ. Sing the song, realizing that the Spirit fills you even as you sing.

Reflecting in Song

This "Celebration Song," with its minor key and strong rhythmic drive, has the style of a Jewish folk song. The song invites physical participation—tambourines, hand clapping, dance. It is most effective when sung several times through, beginning slowly and deliberately, then increasing in tempo and intensity with each succeeding verse. It draws us in with its excitement and exuberance, affirming the joy of coming together with one another in worship.

Corporate worship has been central in the lives of the people of God throughout history, and song has been an integral part of that worship. Throughout the Scriptures, from the "Song of Moses" (Exod. 15) to the "Song of the Lamb" (Rev. 15), God's people gather together and sing praises.

As his people we join in worship not just when we feel joyful, for many times we do not. We worship out of obedience and gratitude. This psalm (149) reminds us, "Praise the Lord! Sing . . . in the assembly of the faithful!" John Wesley reinforces it: "See that you join with the congregation as frequently as you can. Let not a slight degree of weakness or weariness hinder you. If it is a cross to you, take it up, and you will find it a blessing. Sing lustily and with a good courage. Beware of singing as if you were half dead, or half asleep; but lift up your voice with strength."[8] Sing the song again "with a good courage."

When we obey God, blessing follows. When worship brings glory to God, it produces joy in us and it draws others to Christ. Yes, we can certainly worship alone. But together our praises invite a special filling, a powerful anointing of the Spirit. It is just as Jesus promises: "Where two or three are gathered in my name, I am there among them" (Matt. 18:20).

St. Augustine testifies: "How greatly did I weep during hymns and canticles, keenly affected by the voices of your sweet-singing Church! Those voices flowed into my ears, and your truth was distilled into my heart, and from that truth holy emotions overflowed, and the tears ran down, and amid those tears all was well with me."[9] Perhaps you, like Augustine, have felt this tremendous power of Spirit-led, corporate worship. If so, give thanks. Sing the song once again. Celebrate the privilege, the blessing, the joy of gathering "in the presence of your people."

Questions of Examen and Exercises of Devotion

1. Are there times when I have felt less than eager to participate in worship but have done so anyway and found it to be a blessing?
2. Are there times when I have felt less than eager to participate in worship—and haven't?
3. Corporate worship of course does not mean just gathering as a congregation. So plan some times of worship together with a small group or as a family.
4. Consider attending some festival of worship that is different from what you are accustomed to, for example, liturgical festival, Pentecostal praise service, Jewish celebration.

The Prayer of the Heart

O Lord, thank you for the privilege of gathering with your people in worship. Please, let me never take it for granted. Through your Church "may your name be exalted here on earth and in heaven above." Amen.

Fill Me with Your Spirit

Janet L. Janzen

Janet L. Janzen

Quietly

1. Fill me with your Spir - it and take him not a - way.

Fill me with your pow - er to walk in your way.

Fill me with your love, let me love you more to - day.

Fill me, Lord Je - sus, I pray——

2. Guide me with your light,—— let it shine on my way.

Guide me with your truth,—— let me know you more each day.

Take my hand and guide me lest I wan - der a - stray.

Guide me, Lord Je - sus, I pray.—— A—— men.

Accompaniment for this song is found on page 134.

Scripture Reading: Acts 1:1–14, 2:1–13

The birth of the Church of Jesus Christ ushered in by the Holy Spirit is the subject of this passage. As you read, look at what the apostolic band did in preparation: they prayed and they waited. Witness the scene as the Spirit comes—the "violent wind," the tongues of fire, the miraculous speech. See how this work of the Holy Spirit is greeted by the world: with amazement, perplexity, and scorn.

Scripture Meditation: Acts 1:8

But you will receive power when the Holy Spirit has come upon you; and you will be my witnesses in Jerusalem, in all Judea and Samaria, and to the ends of the earth.

These are the last words spoken by Jesus when he was on earth in the flesh. Realize that he speaks them to you even as he did to his disciples. Take time to consider his words. Now, read and pray through this song. Ask God's Spirit to come upon you in a new, refreshing, and powerful way. Quiet your heart, and wait.

Reflecting in Song

Today there is much debate, disagreement, and division in the Church regarding the topic of the Holy Spirit. How sad that we bicker over the parting words of Jesus! How it must grieve him to see us divided over his wonderful gift of the Spirit!

In the midst of the confusion lies one indisputable fact: the Holy Spirit is absolutely essential in our lives. "Be filled with the Spirit," says Paul (Eph. 5:18). This is a continual process—daily fillings, if you will. We may have had extraordinary experiences of being filled in the past, and for those we give thanks. But they are not our source of power today. We cannot say, "Yesterday I experienced the filling of the Spirit, so I have no need today." No, the time to be filled with the Spirit is now. Sing this song, asking him to fill you in a new and living way for today.

Why is the Holy Spirit so essential? Jesus tells us it is so that we may be his witnesses, so that we may show forth his love to the world. This is not something we can do on our own. In *The Church Before the Watching World,* Francis Schaeffer says that in order to be effective witnesses, we must "show forth the love of God and the holiness of God *simultaneously.* If we show either of these without the other, we exhibit not the character, but a caricature of God for the world to see."[10] If we stress love and compassion without holiness and purity, it turns into compromise. If we stress holiness and purity without love and compassion, it is harsh and ugly. We can see this happening all around us in our own lives as well as in our churches and denominations.

In the flesh perhaps we can exhibit the holiness of God *or* the love of God, but to exhibit both simultaneously "we must look *moment by moment* to the work of Christ, to the work of the Holy Spirit."[11] Jesus perfectly embodied both the holiness of God *and* the love of God. By his Spirit, and only by his Spirit, can we do the same in our daily lives.

This is true for me as an individual, and it is true for the Church as a whole. Schaeffer believed that the central problem of our age was "the church of the Lord Jesus Christ, individually or corporately, tending to do the Lord's work in the power of the flesh rather than of the Spirit."[12] What happens when the church operates in the power of the Spirit? We see it in Acts: "The Lord added to their number day by day those who were being saved" (2:47).

May God forgive us for our bickering, our pettiness, our failure to love one another. May Christ send forth his Spirit upon us so that the world may see him in his purity and beauty, his holiness and love. Come, Holy Spirit!

Questions of Examen and Exercises of Devotion

1. Have I in any way contributed to division in the Church regarding the Holy Spirit?
2. Some theologians have said, "One baptism, many fillings." Do you have a position on this issue? Is it important for you to have a position on this issue?
3. Sing this song throughout the week as a prayer for continual filling.
4. Sketch out your next week, considering any ways that the active presence of the Spirit will affect your relationships with family and fellow workers.

The Prayer of the Heart

Lord Jesus, fill me with your Spirit. May I not out of sin or neglect grieve him and drive him away. Help me bring healing to your body and show forth your love and purity to a watching, needy world. Amen.

O Holy Spirit, Enter In

WIE SCHÖN LEUCHTET (8.8.7.8.8.7.4.8.4.8.)

Michael Schirmer, 1640; Tr. Catherine Winkworth, 1863

Philipp Nicolai, 1599

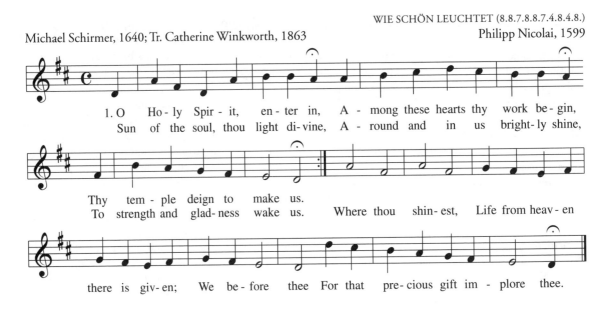

1. O Ho-ly Spir-it, en-ter in, A-mong these hearts thy work be-gin,
Sun of the soul, thou light di-vine, A-round and in us bright-ly shine,

Thy tem-ple deign to make us.
To strength and glad-ness wake us. Where thou shin-est, Life from heav-en

there is giv-en; We be-fore thee For that pre-cious gift im-plore thee.

2. Left to ourselves we shall but stray,
O lead us on the narrow way,
With wisest counsel guide us;
And give us steadfastness, that we
May henceforth truly follow thee,
Whatever woes betide us;
Heal thou gently
Hearts now broken,
Give some token
Thou art near us,
Whom we trust to light and cheer us.

3. O mighty Rock! O Source of life!
Let thy dear word, 'mid doubt and strife,
Be so within us burning,
That we be faithful unto death
In thy pure love and holy faith,
From thee true wisdom learning.
Lord, thy graces
On us shower;
By thy power
Christ confessing,
Let us win his grace and blessing.

4. O gentle Dew from heav'n now fall
With pow'r upon the hearts of all,
Thy tender love instilling,
That heart to heart more closely bound,
In kindly deeds be fruitful found,
The law of love fulfilling;
No wrath, no strife,
Here shall grieve thee,
We receive thee,
Where thou livest,
Peace and love and joy Thou givest.

5. Grant that our days, while life shall last,
In purest holiness be passed;
Our minds so rule and strengthen
That they may rise o'er things of earth,
The hopes and joys that here have birth;
And if our course thou lengthen,
Keep thou pure, Lord,
From offences,
Heart and senses,
Blessed Spirit,
Bid us thus true life inherit.

Scripture Reading: Galatians 5:16–26

"Live by the Spirit," says Paul, and he proceeds to tell us what that means. The word translated here as *live* means literally "go about" or "walk around." If we go about in the Spirit of God, then we will give no opportunity to the flesh. Contrast the works of the flesh with the fruit of the Spirit. Notice that *fruit* is singular; the Spirit-filled life is an integrated, whole life with many different facets, many varieties of fruit.

Scripture Meditation: Galatians 5:22–23

The fruit of the Spirit is love, joy, peace, patience, kindness, generosity, faithfulness, gentleness, and self-control.

As you meditate on this verse, ask the Holy Spirit to affirm which of these has been growing in your life, as well as which you most need at the present time. Then, one at a time, focus on each kind of fruit. Invite God to grow his life in you.

Reflecting in Song

A prayer of invitation to the Holy Spirit, this hymn asks him to come and to do his work, to produce his fruit in our lives. With beautiful poetry and rich content it offers a wealth of material for personal meditation as well as corporate worship. Read through it. Appreciate the language, the poetry, and, above all, the many roles and functions of the Spirit of God.

Coming out of Germany during the tumultuous century following the Reformation, this hymn, like so many others of Germany's greatest and our most enduring hymns, was born in suffering. Michael Schirmer, the author, was a Lutheran poet and teacher who lived through the Thirty Years' War (1618–1648). In ill health most of his life, he also suffered the loss of his wife and two children. Because of the hardship and affliction he endured, Schirmer has been called "the German Job." Philip Nicolai, composer of the melody, was a German Lutheran pastor who also lived under tremendous hardship. A pestilence raged through his village in 1597, claiming 1,300 victims. During that time he wrote a series of meditations entitled "Mirror of Joy" that included a hymn, "How Brightly Beams the Morning Star" ("*Wie schön leuchtet*"), for which he wrote this chorale melody. Known as the "Queen of Chorales," it has been widely used by composers and hymnists alike. Bach used it in six different cantatas.

Sing through the hymn. Every stanza is a prayer in its own right. Pause after each verse to reread and pray to the Holy Spirit: for light and life (v. 1), for guidance and healing (v. 2), for faithfulness and wisdom (v. 3), for love and unity (v. 4), for holiness (v. 5). Be assured that the One who enters and begins this work in you will not leave it unfinished but will bring it to completion.

Questions of Examen and Exercises of Devotion

1. What fruit of the Spirit do I see in the life of someone close to me? What can I do to affirm this quality?

2. What place do I give to the Holy Spirit in my prayer life? Are there changes I might consider?

3. Choose one verse of the hymn that best expresses your needs, your desires, at the moment. Use it in your prayer and meditation for the next few days.

4. Poetry and song are better appropriated by hearing and repeating than by analyzing. Sing this entire hymn every day for a week. Then, be attentive for little phrases, little bits of it to return at unexpected moments as messages from the Holy Spirit. Use these phrases to help you pray for yourself, your church, or others ("Within my heart your work begin . . ."; "Heal thou gently hearts now broken . . .").

The Prayer of the Heart

O Spirit of Jesus, come and do your work within me. And I pray not only for myself but for your Church throughout the world. Give us your light and life, your guidance and healing, your wisdom and grace. May we be holy in life, faithful unto death, bound together in love. Amen.

Spirit Song

SPIRIT SONG (9.7.11.D. with refrain)

John Wimber, 1979

John Wimber, 1979

1. O let the Son of God en-fold you with his Spir-it and his love. Let him fill your heart and sat-is-fy your soul. O let him have the things that hold you, and his Spir-it like a dove will de-scend up-on your life and make you whole.

2. O come and sing this song with glad-ness as your hearts are filled with joy. Lift your hands in sweet sur-ren-der to his name. O give him all your tears and sad-ness; give him all your years of pain, and you'll en-ter in-to life in Je-sus' name.

Refrain

Je-sus, O Je-sus, come and fill your lambs.

Je-sus, O Je-sus, come and fill your lambs.

Accompaniment for this song is found on page 136.

Scripture Reading: Isaiah 61:1–4, Luke 4:14–21

The words of the prophet Isaiah are quoted or referred to throughout the New Testament and especially in the Gospels. In this instance Jesus leaves no doubt that these words apply to him. Observe that the passage in Isaiah takes the form of a song. It is Isaiah's Spirit song.

Scripture Meditation: Isaiah 61:1–3a

The spirit of the Lord GOD is upon me,
  because the LORD has anointed me;
he has sent me to bring good news to the oppressed,
  to bind up the brokenhearted,
to proclaim liberty to the captives,
  and release to the prisoners;
to proclaim the year of the LORD's favor,
  and the day of vengeance of our God;
  to comfort all who mourn;
to provide for those who mourn in Zion—
  to give them a garland instead of ashes,
the mantle of praise instead of a faint spirit.

Receive this message of hope and healing, freedom and release. Center in on each of these phrases, one at a time. Be sensitive to any phrase that may speak especially to you, addressing a current need. Allow the Spirit of God to speak this phrase into your heart, into your soul.

Reflecting in Song

This song expresses the healing, wholeness, and freedom we have in Jesus through his Spirit. It is a song of surrendering our lives, of letting him fill us and fulfill us. The song was written by John Wimber, a former Las Vegas band leader who is now a pastor and head of Vineyard Ministries International. Wimber has had worldwide influence in the contemporary church renewal movement. He continues to write Christian music, and "Spirit Song" has become known in mainline denominations as well as in charismatic circles.

Read through the first verse. Consider "the things that hold you." They may be material or spiritual things; they may be relationships; they may be memories or anxieties, grief or guilt. Ask the Holy Spirit to show you what they are. Offer them up to him. Now sing this verse and rest in his sufficiency. Know that this Spirit who comes gently "like a dove" brings healing in his wings (Mal. 4:2). Let him heal you and make you whole.

Elisabeth Elliot says that "every experience, if offered up to Jesus, can be your gateway to joy."[13] Read

the second verse and call to mind your "tears and sadness . . . your years of pain." They may be the tears and pain of a victim. Give them to God as much as you are able. Be assured that nothing offered to him is ever wasted. He "will repay you for the years that the swarming locust has eaten" (Joel 2:25). Yours may be tears and pain brought on by your own disobedience. No matter. "All things work together for our good, even our sins and vices," says George MacDonald. "[Christ] defeats our sins, makes them prisoners, forces them into the service of good, and chains them like galley slaves to the rowing benches of the gospel ship."[14] He who brings life from death also brings joy from sorrow, good from evil. Sing the second verse and release your pain and tears, your sin and fears to the Holy Spirit. Allow this Comforter to do his work. Let him free you as you "enter into life in Jesus' name."

Sing the entire song once again, focusing on the refrain. Remember that "filling" does not depend upon "feeling." We are filled with the Spirit in the same way that we are saved—by faith. Believe him who says, "If you . . . know how to give good gifts to your children, how much more will the heavenly Father give the Holy Spirit to those who ask him!" (Luke 11:13). Ask! Receive! Believe! Now, thank God for the fullness of his Spirit.

Questions of Examen and Exercises of Devotion

1. In what ways has the Holy Spirit been my healer? My liberator?
2. Has there been an experience of sorrow or suffering in my life that God has transformed into a "gateway to joy"?
3. Today, perhaps now, lift your hands in sweet surrender to Jesus' name.
4. In her book *Showings,*[15] Julian of Norwich (1343–1413) uses phrases like "enfolded in love" and "enfolded in the goodness of God," which match wonderfully with the opening words of "Spirit Song." Read several passages from *Showings* with this song as a backdrop and see what you learn.

The Prayer of the Heart

Thank you, Jesus, for your Spirit who loves and comforts, fills and frees. I give you the things that hold me captive. I give you my tears, my sorrows, my pain. Thank you for filling me with your life-giving Spirit. Thank you for your love, which redeems all. Amen.

Joy to the World

ANTIOCH (C.M. with repeats)

Isaac Watts, 1719

Lowell Mason, 1848; based on G. F. Handel, 1742

1. Joy to the world! the Lord is come; Let earth re-
2. Joy to the earth! the Sav-ior reigns; Let men their
3. No more let sins and sor-rows grow, Nor thorns in-
4. He rules the world with truth and grace, And makes the

ceive her King; Let ev-ery heart pre-pare Him room,
songs em-ploy; While fields and floods, rocks, hills, and plains
fest the ground; He comes to make His bless-ings flow
na-tions prove The glo-ries of His right-eous-ness,

And heav'n and na-ture sing, And heav'n and na-ture
Re-peat the sound-ing joy, Re-peat the sound-ing
Far as the curse is found, Far as the curse is
And won-ders of His love, And won-ders of His

1. And heav'n and na-ture sing,

1. And

sing, And heav'n, and heav'n and na-ture sing.
joy, Re-peat, re-peat the sound-ing joy.
found, Far as, far as the curse is found.
love, And won-ders, won-ders of His love.

heav'n and na-ture sing,

Scripture Reading: Psalm 98

The Psalms have been a part of the worship of God's people since the time of David. In the Hebrew tradition it was common to sing them antiphonally, that is, in two groups with one responding to the other. Read this psalm aloud. See how it lends itself to antiphonal use. Imagine a congregation singing these phrases back and forth to one another with growing excitement and jubilation. Read the psalm again. Notice how the first part recounts God's mighty acts while the second part (vv. 4–9) calls forth a response of praise from all creation.

Scripture Meditation: Psalm 98:4

Make a joyful noise to the LORD, all the earth;
break forth into joyous song and sing praises.

After reading this verse, close your eyes and repeat it several times from memory. Now sing "Joy to the World." Think of joy resounding throughout the creation as you join a mighty chorus of humanity and nature, heaven and earth in singing praises to God.

Reflecting in Song

No doubt you are immediately reminded of Christmas when you sing this hymn. It is a wonderful Christmas carol, but it is so much more! Too often we limit our appreciation of a song because certain associations have developed around it either in our own experience or in our culture. Such is the case with "Joy to the World." This hymn was written by Isaac Watts not as a Christmas carol but as a paraphrase of Psalm 98:4–9.

Watts grew up in seventeenth-century England at a time when only psalms were sung in worship, and those were often not done very well. A contemporary of Watts wrote of the "whining, tooting, yelling, or screeching" taking place in many congregations.[16] One day in church when the eighteen year old expressed his disgust at the singing and refused to participate, his father suggested that if Isaac were smarter than King David, then perhaps he should write something better. Watts's first hymn was sung the following Sunday, and he eventually wrote over six hundred more. In so doing, he ushered in a new era of hymn singing in England and became known as the "Father of English Hymnody."[17] Many of Watts' hymns are still considered among the finest in the English language.

In his psalm paraphrases, Watts's goal was "to make David speak like a Christian." Read through the song and see how Watts has Christianized this psalm.

Sing the first two verses. Contemplate the phrase, "the Lord *is* come." He is indeed—Emmanuel, God with us. This is the good news of the gospel! The evangelistic call is for each of us to "prepare him room" not just at Advent or Christmas but every day.

This hymn celebrates the incarnation, the Word become flesh, breaking the power of sin and bringing God's kingdom to human hearts. But it also celebrates with prophetic vision Jesus' return in glory. Sing the last two verses and catch this vision.

All of creation has finally come under Christ's Lordship. The physical curse of sin is broken, and creation is free from its bondage at last (Rom. 8:21). Sorrow and suffering are things of the past. Jesus rules "with truth and grace," and his kingdom of righteousness, peace, and joy is now a manifest reality. Joy to the world!

Questions of Examen and Exercises of Devotion

1. Where in my life do I need to prepare him room?
2. What "wonders of his love" have I experienced recently?
3. Memorize all the verses of "Joy to the World."
4. Next time you hear this hymn in a store or a mall, pause and repeat, "The Lord is come!" Thank him that he is there with you, and pray for those around you that they may know the joy of his presence.

The Prayer of the Heart

Lord Jesus, Emmanuel, thank you that you are here. I open my heart and ask that you show me today an area where you should have more room. May your joy echo throughout my heart and life so that you always may be glorified. Amen.

The Trees of the Field

Steffi Geiser Rubin; based on Isaiah 55:12

Stuart Dauermann

With spirit

You shall go out with joy and be led forth with peace; The moun-tains and the hills will break forth be-fore you. There'll be shouts of joy and all the trees of the field will clap, will clap their hands. And all the trees of the field will clap their hands, The trees of the field will clap their hands, The trees of the field will clap their hands While you go out with joy.

Scripture Reading: Isaiah 55

In this Scripture God offers to "everyone who thirsts" refreshment, satisfaction, and abundant life. They are freely available to all who will "come," "seek," "return." The passage concludes with a glorious procession of the redeemed. Notice the joyous celebration of nature as it shares in the promised redemption.

Scripture Meditation: Isaiah 55:12 (KJV)

For ye shall go out with joy, and be led forth with peace: the mountains and the hills shall break forth before you into singing, and all the trees of the field shall clap their hands.

Reflect upon this—God's promise to you as one of his redeemed. Consider how the joy and peace of Christ are a present reality. Ponder the time to come when Christ's kingdom is revealed and the people of God joyfully enter the New Jerusalem, as all creation—the "new heavens and new earth"—rejoices! Sing this song in celebration.

Reflecting in Song

Throughout Scripture and especially in the Psalms, the rejoicing creation—heavens and earth, mountains and seas, animals and trees—unites to praise God. In this exuberant song of Isaiah we see a vivid picture of mountains singing and trees clapping their hands. Figurative language? Perhaps, as it applies to the present time. But there are indications, besides this verse, that this "singing creation" might actually come to pass. Isaiah writes, "Sing, O heavens, for the Lord has done it. . . . Break forth into singing, O mountains, O forest, and every tree in it! For the Lord has redeemed Jacob, and will be glorified in Israel" (44:23). David refers to a time when "the trees of the forest sing for joy before the LORD" (1 Chron. 16:33).

Philosophers of the past understood song as being at the heart of creation. "The very universe . . . is held together by a certain harmony of sounds," said the sixth-century philosopher Isidore of Seville.[18] Contemporary composer Alice Parker observes, "Some scientists speak of vibration as at the heart of all physical processes, so it may be literally true that 'All nature sings.'"[19] Might not this music some day be made manifest? Sing again, and enter into this song of creation.

If even the rocks and trees are to voice God's praise, how much more will every living thing join in! In Revelation 5:13, John witnesses: "Then I heard every creature in heaven and on earth and under the earth and in the sea, and all that is in them, singing . . . 'to the Lamb be blessing and honor and glory and might forever and ever!'" "What can this mean," asks Elisabeth Elliot, "if not that in some way unimaginable to us now . . . all feathered, furred, scaled, and carapaced creatures will be redeemed? . . . Will not our ears someday hear the Song of the Animals? I think so."[20]

As of yet, nature "groans in travail," unable to articulate its praise. But a day will come when "sorrow and sighing shall flee" and all creation will break forth into jubilant song, dance, and celebration. The curse of thorn and brier, tooth and claw will be broken as even the wolf and the lamb rejoice together. How exciting—to anticipate all creation finally reconciled, fully alive, able to sing God's praise at last! No wonder creation "waits with eager longing for the revealing of the children of God" (Rom. 8:19)! Repeat the song a few more times, adding physical expressions such as clapping or dancing and increasing the tempo on each repetition. Join in the anticipation of that wonder-filled day of redemption.

Questions of Examen and Exercises of Devotion

1. Are there things that hinder my full participation in the sentiment of this song?
2. Are joy and peace dominant characteristics of my life? Why or why not?
3. Share in the praises of nature through these Scriptures: Job 38:4–7; Psalm 19:1–4, 84:3–4, 148.
4. Explore further the promised redemption of nature in these passages: Isaiah 11:6–9, 65:17–25; Romans 8:18–25; 2 Peter 3:13–14; Revelation 21:1–4.

The Prayer of the Heart

O Lord, today may the rhythm in my feet and the music in my soul be a prayer of praise to you. Amen.

Songs of Shalom

When we commit injustice we are without music.

—*Cassiodorus*

The life pleasing to God is not a set of pious exercises for the devout but a trumpet call to a freely gathered, martyr people who will bring the life and powers of the kingdom of God to bear upon the pressing social issues of our day. Love of God, of necessity, drives us into love of neighbor; and love of neighbor, of necessity, leads us to the bruised and broken of the earth.

Once we see the misery of the oppressed, we are called to champion their cause and plead for justice. Before authorities we become the voice of the voiceless, the face of the faceless. In all places and in all ways we seek peace and justice, compassion and service, reconciliation and community.

As St. Francis did so long ago, we become instruments of God's peace, sowing

love where there is hatred,
healing where there is injury,
faith where there is doubt,
hope were there is despair,
light where there is darkness,
and joy where there is grief.

We Pray for Peace

Ken Medema

Ken Medema

We pray for peace, for peace a-mong the na - tions.

We pray for peace, good-will a-mong the peo - ple.

'Til love comes down like a sum-mer rain; 'til the riv-ers of jus-tice

flow a - gain, 'til the day of ju-bi - lee is come,

We pray for peace up - on our plan - et home.

Accompaniment for this song is found on page 138.

Scripture Reading: Isaiah 11:1–9

This is one of the great messianic passages in the Bible. Notice the all-encompassing nature of the prophetic word: with Messiah comes peace to the natural world and reconciliation between the human creation and the animal creation. This passage has been the inspiration for a famous painting entitled *The Peaceable Kingdom.* Many have debated the question of how much of this prophetic message is relevant to this present age and how much is reserved for the age to come. What do you think?

Scripture Meditation: Isaiah 11:9

This meditation text sums up the hope of all humanity:

> *They will not hurt or destroy*
> *on all my holy mountain;*
> *for the earth will be full of the knowledge of the LORD*
> *as the waters cover the sea.*

Allow the text to merge with the song. Read and sing, read and sing, until an overall impression of wholeness and reconciliation and *shalom* emerges into your consciousness. Stay with the Scripture text until the impression becomes clearly defined, even if that should take some weeks.

Reflecting in Song

In our day peace seems so elusive, so easily shattered by the harsh realities of the modern world. But remember, the peaceable kingdom of our God and of his Christ has always been a hard reality to hold on to—even in Isaiah's day. But in spite of everything Isaiah held on to a vision of God's righteous rule, and so should we. So in the midst of what appear to be insurmountable odds, we pray for peace.

Right here many stumble. Prayer seems too ethereal, too weak, too powerless to have much impact upon a world of warfare and bloodshed. What can prayer do against guns and missiles, tanks and warplanes? In this we simply misunderstand the nature of prayer; it allows us to tap into a spiritual reality that dwarfs all the weapons systems of modern technology. The prayer for peace, tied as it is to a longing for goodwill among all people, unleashes a torrent of love and justice that cannot be stopped. To the natural eye it appears as a weak weapon, but in the unseen world forces are at work that will in the end win out. The ocean of love and light ultimately conquers the ocean of darkness and death.

Therefore sing—and pray—with confidence for peace to come upon our planet home. And then join in the jubilee that is coming to birth in our midst.

Questions of Examen and Exercises of Devotion

1. Do I work for peace in all human relationships and social structures?
2. Is there anyone in my circle of nearness that I could like more?
3. Identify one or two specific places in the world where hatred abounds. Then bathe those places in prayer for a month or more.
4. Undertake an experiment in *ora et labora,* prayer and work. Find some task for peace and work at it, praying as you work and through the work.

The Prayer of the Heart

> *O Lord, so open my eyes and my ears*
> *that I may this coming day be able to do some work of*
> *peace for thee. Amen.*

—Alan Paton

Down by the Riverside

Traditional Spiritual   Traditional Spiritual

1. Gon-na lay down my sword and shield, Down by the riv-er-side, Down by the riv-er-side, Down by the riv-er-side; Gon-na lay down my sword and shield, Down by the riv-er-side, Gon-na stud-y war no more.

Refrain
I ain'-a gon-na stud-y war no more, ain'-a gon-na stud-y war no more, ain'-a gon-na stud-y war no more. I ain'-a gon-na stud-y war no more, ain'-a gon-na stud-y war no more, Ain'-a gon-na stud-y war no more.

2. Gonna lay down my burden, Down by the riverside . . .
3. Gonna try on my starry crown, Down by the riverside . . .
4. Gonna meet my dear old father, Down by the riverside . . .
5. Gonna meet my dear old mother, Down by the riverside . . .
6. Gonna meet my loving Jesus, Down by the riverside . . .

Scripture Reading: Isaiah 2:1–4

In this Scripture is a great vision of peoples from every nation streaming to Zion, the mountain of God. It is a wonderful description of reconciliation and justice among the nations. Instead of differences being settled by bloody battle, the Lord judges among the nations.

Swords are beaten into plowshares and spears into pruning hooks—what a glorious, hope-filled vision!

Scripture Meditation: Isaiah 2:4b

Begin your meditation by singing the first verse of this well-known spiritual. Allow the refrain to become a personal affirmation and confession; "I ain'a gonna study war no more." Now, memorize the text:

> They shall beat their swords into plowshares,
> and their spears into pruning hooks;
> nation shall not lift up sword against nation,
> neither shall they learn war any more.

Allow prayers to rise from your heart for the fulfillment of this vision. Pray for the nations. Pray for the collapse of hostilities between peoples. Pray for the peace of the cities. Imagine swords and shields and B-1 bombers and Trident missile systems all melted down and turned into plowshares and pruning hooks and medical technology and recreation equipment.

Reflecting in Song

The spiritual is an original African American contribution to music. Born as it was out of terrible anguish and bondage, it reaches into our hearts and souls in unexplainable ways. No other form of music touches us quite like the spiritual. It has a mysterious way of awakening those longings that lie buried deep within us all.

Among the powerful characteristics of the spiritual are the repetitive refrains and responses, which allow for considerable improvisation. Words can be freely changed, responded to, and added on to as the singer is taken up into the message of the song.[1]

Personally, I (Richard) will always remember the use of this particular song in a gathering of young Quakers from across North America. We had been struggling with the hard issues of war and peace, earnestly trying to cut through the Gordian knot of the conflict in Southeast Asia. Then in the midst of our debate and our struggle, someone began singing, "Gonna lay down my sword and shield, down by the riverside. . . ." The song began to move throughout the group, first in a quiet, almost tentative way, then with greater and greater conviction. Time seemed to stand still as dozens upon dozens of verses were improvised. ("Gonna lay down my napalm bomb . . .") Our resolve grew and deepened. In those days we were a few lonely voices crying in the wilderness, but in time the conscience of an entire nation was aroused, and a tumultuous cry went forth (accompanied by many unsavory influences) that could not be ignored.

Perhaps you will want to reflect on some contemporary issue to which this song can speak a prophetic word. Then sing with that situation and issue as a backdrop. This may even draw you into improvising appropriate verses.

The backdrop to the riverside imagery is the crossing over Jordan and entering the promised land. This metaphor is used to refer both to our living in the fullness of the kingdom of God now and our transition from this life into the greater life of heaven. With this in mind, consider first what burdens you are carrying that you need to lay down. Try to identify specific burdens. Then, as you sing, let go of each one. Make up verses that name the burdens.

Next, consider your death. (It will come, you know, and it is best to come to terms with this reality of human existence.) Notice how many of the verses to this song view this crossing over Jordan as a reunion, a meeting of those who have gone on before. Recently a brother of mine died, and as we were saying good-bye to each other, I asked him to be sure to greet our parents for me and the baby sister who died in childbirth. This is one of the great hopes of heaven. Death, which takes away our friends and loved ones, will one day restore to us what it took away, for we, too, will cross over Jordan. Sing this spiritual thinking of—even naming—those you hope to meet someday soon—not only family but those in the larger family of faith. Such is the hope of the resurrection: because he lives, we too shall live.

Questions of Examen and Exercises of Devotion

1. Are there aspects of Isaiah's great vision of reconciliation that I dislike?
2. Am I afraid to deal with the topic of death?
3. Assuming that you made a conscious choice to "study war no more," jot down a list of things you might study instead.
4. Go to an actual riverside and use it as a visual backdrop for the singing of this spiritual.

The Prayer of the Heart

Lord, laying things down is not my style. I like to pick things up—to be in charge, to accomplish. Help me to know what to lay down and what to pick up so that I may ever live in harmony with your ways. Amen.

Let Justice Roll

Ken Medema

Ken Medema

With passion

Let jus-tice roll, roll down like wa-ter, and right-cous-ness like a flow-ing stream. Let jus-tice roll, roll down like wa-ter, and right-eous-ness like a flow-ing stream. It's a call to leave your trea-sures and your trin-kets on the road. It's a call to join the weep-ing, and to bear the suf-ferer's load. It's a call to be the low-ly, it's a call to be the least. It's a call to join the fast-ing that shall lead to fi-nal feast. Let jus-tice roll, roll down like wa-ter, and right-eous-ness like a flow-ing stream. Let jus-tice roll, roll like the wa-ter, and right-eous-ness like a flow-ing stream.

Accompaniment for this song is found on page 140.

Scripture Reading: Amos 5:18–24

As you read this passage, consider God's utter disdain for injustice—whether in Amos's day or our own. Note the use of words like *hate* and *despise*—words we seldom associate with God but words that are eminently appropriate when describing his attitude toward oppression.

"The day of the Lord" was believed to be a great time of liberation and rejoicing, but, as this passage makes clear, it is a fearful day of terrible judgment for all who "sell the needy for a pair of shoes and trample the head of the poor" (Amos 2:6–7). For all of us these words are a sober warning to live in such a way that "the day of the Lord" can be welcomed rather than dreaded.

Scripture Meditation: Amos 5:24

Since this song quotes the Scripture text almost verbatim, begin your meditation by singing it, allowing the music to carry the words into your mind and heart. Now dwell on the text:

> *But let justice roll down like waters,*
> *and righteousness like an ever-flowing stream.*

What would it look like for great waves of justice and righteousness to flood into your community, workplace, and home? How would it alter attitudes at work? What changes would it make in your assessment of those who are marginalized by our society?

Reflecting in Song

The Hebrew words for justice and righteousness (*mishpat* and *tsedaqah*) are massive words. They encompass God's concern for the bruised and the broken. They speak of the primacy of action, so that our performance outstrips our profession. This song by Ken Medema, a blind and highly gifted contemporary composer, drives home these powerful words by means of rhythm and repetition. Sing the refrain over several times. Let the concerns for justice and righteousness grow and deepen with each repetition.

Now, look at the middle part of the song. Notice its strong call to commitment. In fact, it uses the word *call* four times. Consider each call in the light of your personal situation.

The call to leave treasures and trinkets: What might this refer to in your life?

The call to join the weeping and to bear the sufferer's load: Who in your circle of friendships are carrying especially heavy loads right now? Who in your society?

The call to be the lowly and the least: Notice this is a summons not merely to associate with the lowly, but *to be* the lowly. How is this done? Is it even desirable?

The call to a fasting that leads to feasting: Are you open to fasting as a Christian spiritual discipline? What besides food might that involve?

Once more sing the song through in its entirety, watching for any emotions or thoughts that surface. See if you can identify and clarify them, especially as regards any specific action you are being asked to undertake.

Questions of Examen and Exercises of Devotion

1. Have I in any way neglected the poor and needy?
2. When have I deliberately sought out the weak and powerless?
3. For one month consider doing all your shopping in an economically depressed section of your city.
4. Spend one afternoon with the homeless or unemployed, listening to their stories.

The Prayer of the Heart

Lord, I confess that it is easier for me to make offerings and have solemn assemblies than to do simple justice for the poor. I have allowed society to hide the poor from me. Forgive, O Lord, forgive. May I become aware of those who labor for me out of my sight. Amen.

Prayer of St. Francis

Attr. to St. Francis of Assisi (1182–1226)
Paraphrased by Janet L. Janzen

Janet L. Janzen

1. Make me an in-stru-ment of Thy peace, O Lord, this is my prayer._____ Where there is hat-red, let me sow love, And by grace may it grow there._____

2. May I bring heal-ing for in-jur-y done, And faith where doubt would de-stroy,_____ Hope for des-pair,_____ light in the dark, And in grief may I sow joy._____

3. Grant that I may not live un-to my-self, O Mas-ter, this is my plea;_____ May I give un-der-stand-ing, com-fort and love Un-to all as un-to Thee._____

Refrain

For it is in giv-ing that we re-ceive,

And it is in par-don-ing that we are freed,

And it is in dy-ing that we are born

Coda (last time only)

to live e-ter-nal-ly._____ To live e-ter-nal-ly._____

Accompaniment for this song is found on page 142.

Scripture Reading: Romans 6:5–14

As you read this passage, follow the logic of Paul's argument of death and resurrection that free us from the dominion of sin. As a result, we can yield our bodily members up to God as instruments of righteousness.

Scripture Meditation: Romans 6:13

No longer present your members to sin as instruments of wickedness, but present yourselves to God as those who have been brought from death to life, and present your members to God as instruments of righteousness.

Pause at each phrase of this passage. Consider the ways in the past that you have presented your hands, feet, tongue, and so forth to sin as instruments of wickedness; how you have been brought from death to life; and the ways you can now present your hands, feet, tongue, and so forth to God as instruments of righteousness.

Reflecting in Song

Sing or read through this song. It is a new musical paraphrase of the famous prayer attributed to St. Francis of Assisi.[2] This prayer emphasizes peace and reconciliation through self-sacrifice. A key word used here—*instrument*—can have several different meanings ("Make me an instrument of Thy peace.") In Romans 6:13 Paul uses the word *instrument* to refer to a weapon. Using this understanding in the context of the prayer means that we are to be "weapons of peace." This kind of instrument is active, not passive. It is on the offensive, working for peace, for justice, for *shalom*. It can work only in the power of the Spirit, in concert with the "whole armor of God" (Eph. 6:10–18). Paradoxically, its strength is made perfect in weakness, in surrender, and in obedience to the will of God.

St. Francis's whole prayer is a paradox. It shows us how in God's economy everything is upside down. Jesus set the example for us, and the Little Poor Man of Assisi followed in his footsteps. His prayer illustrates this upside-down life in the kingdom of God. In the world we strive for our rights; in the kingdom we relinquish what we believe we deserve and seek the lowly place. In the world we strive for power; in the kingdom we embrace a life of service. In the world we strive for self-fulfillment; in the kingdom we die to ourselves.

But these are not negative things. Francis himself is known for his joy and most of all as one who overflowed with love—love for God, love for people, and love for every part of God's creation. These are the things that make for peace.

Now, sing this song again, giving special attention to the refrain. Reflect on how contrary its teaching is to the dominant mood of our day. And yet the words are so true. Think of times in your life when you found it true that giving led to receiving, that pardoning brought you freedom, that dying to self gave you new life. In the light of these great truths, dedicate yourself to live, like St. Francis, against the tide of contemporary culture.

Questions of Examen and Exercises of Devotion

1. Where have I injured others or witnessed injury done? Are there things I can do to bring healing?
2. Are there ways I can be an instrument of peace at my work or among my neighbors?
3. This week, for the sake of another, give up something to which you feel you have a right. Ask God to bring life out of it.
4. Forgive someone who has injured you. Use the Prayer of St. Francis to seek God's help.

The Prayer of the Heart

Lord Jesus, the world is so filled with destruction. I despair at it and I condemn it. And yet I too take part in its destructive ways—belittling, defaming, slandering. Have mercy, O Lord! Forgive, O Lord! Make me an instrument of your peace. Amen.

Whatever You Do
(four-part round)

Janet L. Janzen; based on Matthew 25:40

Janet L. Janzen

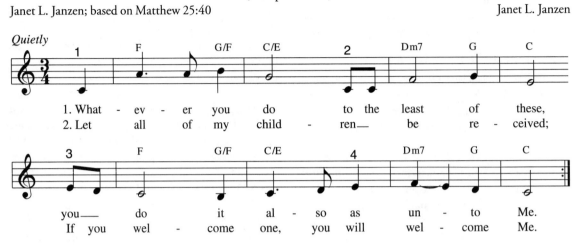

1. What - ev - er you do to the least of these,
2. Let all of my child - ren— be re - ceived;

you— do it al - so as un - to Me.
If you wel - come one, you will wel - come Me.

Scripture Reading: Matthew 25:31–46

This passage gives a picture of the time to come when the Son of Man returns and judges the earth. Notice the criteria by which he separates the sheep from the goats. It is those who have served the very basic needs of others—both physical and emotional—who receive the reward. Simple acts of obedience done in the name of Christ and for his sake are not forgotten by him.

Scripture Meditation: Matthew 25:40

Truly I tell you, just as you did it to one of the least of these who are members of my family, you did it to me.

Let these words of Jesus speak directly to you. Repeat them. Listen to them. Recall how you have served Christ by serving one of his "least" this past week. Ask him to show you where you have failed and to make you more aware of "the least of these."

Reflecting in Song

Jesus attaches great importance to "little things." "Let the little children come to me," he says, "for it is to such as these that the kingdom of heaven belongs" (Matt. 19:14). Small, unpretentious actions have eternal ramifications: "Whoever gives to one of these little ones even a cup of cold water . . . shall not lose his reward" (Matt. 10:42, RSV). And whoever is faithful in little will be trusted with much (Luke 19:17). The kingdom of God is made up of the least, the last, the smallest—things and people overlooked or scorned by the rest of the world.

This short, simple song is about "the least of these." Each verse is intended to be sung in several repetitions so that it can be assimilated before moving on to the next verse. The song can also be sung as a round. Sing it now and become familiar with it.

Now, look once again at the Scripture passage and pay particular attention to the things done by those who were rewarded. These are not profound "spiritual" things, great sacrifices, or extraordinary deeds. These are little things in life—ordinary, everyday things like feeding one who is hungry, welcoming a stranger, caring for one who is sick. We do not need to look far for opportunities to do any of these; they lie close at hand. Each of us could do one of these things this very day. Sing the song again. Consider your opportunities today.

Life is made up of little things—little things that are of eternal importance. We do them, not because they add up to something bigger or because they earn salvation in any way. We do them out of obedience and out of love for Jesus and because nothing is little in the eyes of God. We will not always know the significance of these little things. A kind word to a child, a note or call to one who is lonely, a "cup of cold water" given in the name of Christ—all may have a dramatic, lasting effect in someone's life.

George MacDonald says, "Simple obedience—treating everyone you encounter as Christ would treat him, in the next five minutes, all your life long—will do more to further the coming of God's true kingdom, than all you could do with a million pounds, were it handed you to spend 'in his work' the moment you finish this sentence."[3] Small acts of kindness and courtesy, compassion and hospitality carry eternal weight. Lives are changed—and the world is changed—by little things. With these realities in mind, sing the song once again.

Questions of Examen and Exercises of Devotion

1. What "little thing" done by someone else has made a lasting difference in my life?
2. Who are "the least of these" in my life? In our society? In the world? How might I meet a simple need or do an act of kindness for one of them?
3. Choose one act of kindness you can do today for each person who lives with you, for example, a note of appreciation, a chore to lighten a burden, and so forth.
4. Pick one day this week and make a conscious attempt to give special dignity to everyone you encounter "in the next five minutes"—whether on the phone, on the freeway, or in the checkout line.

The Prayer of the Heart

Dear Lord, give me the insight to recognize those who are most vulnerable and helpless in my world and the will to be a help to them. Amen.

Simple Gifts

Shaker Song

Shaker Song

'Tis the gift to be sim - ple, 'tis the gift to be free, 'Tis the

gift to come down where we ought to be, And when we find our - selves in the

place just right, 'Twill be in the val - ley of love and de - light.

When true sim - pli - ci - ty is gained, To bow and to bend we shan't be a - shamed, To

turn, turn, will be our de - light, Till by turn - ing, turn - ing we come round right.

Scripture Reading: Matthew 6:19–34 (RSV)

When you read this passage, notice how many of the concerns of daily life in Jesus' time—food, clothing, possessions—were the same as those we face today. The Greek word for "sound" used in verse 22 in reference to the eye also means "simple" or "single." Consider how you in your world can follow Jesus' emphasis on singleness of purpose: *one* focus, *one* master, *one* goal.

Scripture Meditation: Matthew 6:33

> *But seek first his kingdom and his righteousness, and all these things shall be yours as well.*

Contemplate these words of Jesus. Enter an experience of being pared down to this single reality. Let go of the mundane duties and cares of life that are preoccupying you. Let go of the major problems and worries that are plaguing you. Focus on the kingdom of God and his righteousness. Think on the King of kings, Christ Jesus, who is himself the righteousness of God.

Reflecting in Song

Sing through this old Shaker song and enter into its joyful, carefree spirit. Shakers would often dance to this song, celebrating the gift of simplicity, a wonderfully freeing gift leading to "the valley of love and delight." Our word *simple,* derived from the Latin word meaning "single," sometimes has negative or austere connotations. Singing this song can help us regain a right perspective on the gift and discipline of simplicity.

Simplicity has never been easy because, as A. W. Tozer reminds us, ever since the fall the gifts of God have usurped the place of God and "within the human heart, things have taken over."[4] We may rationalize this reality, saying that our age is more complicated than any other. But our Scripture shows us that life has always been complicated. Possessions have always required time and effort to protect. Food and clothing have always been daily concerns. Some worry where their next meal is coming from, while others worry about how many grams of fat there are in breakfast cereal. Technology, prosperity, and political freedom increase our choices. But this does not excuse us from practicing simplicity. On the contrary, it makes our need for it all the more acute.

The practice of simplicity, of course, extends beyond possessions. There is a need for simplicity in our schedules. Do we "seek first his kingdom" before we write in our datebooks? Can we enjoy simple entertainment—reading, walking, singing? There is the simplicity of personality—ridding ourselves of pretense and seeking to bless rather than to impress. Can we accept "the gift to come down where we ought to be"?

There is such a thing as simple faith. This is not simplistic faith, which asks no questions. It is childlike faith, which, though full of questions, trusts in a wise, loving Father. Simplicity is needed in every area of our lives.

How can we go about receiving and practicing this gift of simplicity? It begins with singularity or simplicity of heart. It involves turning and returning, again and again, to our single focus; to always "seek first his kingdom and his righteousness."

Questions of Examen and Exercises of Devotion

1. Have I set any goals that rival my "seeking first his kingdom"?
2. What complications or distractions are hindering my single focus today? What should I do about them?
3. Before making your next major purchase, ask yourself what complications it might add to your life.
4. Practice simplicity of speech by resisting the temptation to justify yourself one time each day this week.

The Prayer of the Heart

Lord Jesus, so many things have a hold on my heart. I give them to you and ask for grace and mercy. Give me in return the gift of simplicity so I can say with the psalmist, "There is nothing on earth that I desire other than You" (Ps. 73:25). Amen.

This Is My Father's World

Maltbie D. Babcock, 1901

TERRA BEATA (6.6.8.6.D)
Franklin L. Sheppard, 1915

1. This is my Fa-ther's world, And to my lis-tening ears
All na-ture sings, and round me rings The mu-sic of the spheres.
This is my Fa-ther's world, I rest me in the thought
Of rocks and trees, of skies and seas; His hand the won-ders wrought.

2. This is my Father's world,
   The birds their carols raise;
   The morning light, the lily white
   Declare their Maker's praise.
   This is my Father's world,
   He shines in all that's fair;
   In the rustling grass I hear Him pass,
   He speaks to me everywhere.

3. This is my Father's world,
   O let me ne'er forget
   That though the wrong seems oft so strong,
   God is the ruler yet.
   This is my Father's world,
   Why should my heart be sad?
   The Lord is King; Let the heavens ring!
   God reigns; Let the earth be glad!

Scripture Reading: Psalm 148

This psalm calls upon all of creation to give praise to God. Observe how the first six verses speak to the inhabitants of the heavens, describing the reasons for them to praise God. The next eight verses address the inhabitants of the earth—everyone and everything from kings to children to cattle to mountains and fruit trees.

Scripture Meditation: Psalm 148:13

Begin by singing this hymn. Repeat the final line: "The Lord is king; let the heavens ring! God reigns; Let the earth be glad!" Notice how it sums up Psalm 148. You may want to memorize this meditation text:

> Let them praise the name of the LORD,
>   for his name alone is exalted;
>   his glory is above earth and heaven.

Reflecting in Song

"This is my *Father's* world!" This simple phrase offers the most compelling reason for Christians to be compassionate caretakers of the earth. Those who know God as Father want to help protect his creation. It is more than acting as faithful stewards—it is the response of loving sons and daughters.

Dr. Maltbie D. Babcock, the author of this hymn, had a great love for God's creation. Setting forth on his early morning walks through the hills of upstate New York, he would often announce, "I'm going out to see my Father's world."

Look at the first verse of his song. Notice how it focuses on the great wonders of nature—stars and planets, skies and seas. The "music of the spheres," mentioned here, was a common theme of the ancient philosophers. Aristotle described it as the "harmony produced by all the heavenly bodies singing and dancing together."[5] Perhaps one day we will actually hear this heavenly music, which is as yet beyond the range of human ears.

Now look at the second verse. Sing it. Notice how it centers on small things—birds, lilies, grass. Small, but significant. You may remember that these are the same things Jesus referred to when dealing with human anxiety (Matt. 6:25–34). These creatures, too, give forth constant praise to God. Some, like the birds, sing audibly, while others, such as the lily, declare his praise visibly. Ask God to give you ears and eyes for this great paean of praise. Through these small wonders let him speak to you everywhere.

Turn your attention now to verse three and sing it. Our Father's world is a tragically fallen world—a "good world gone bad" as C. S. Lewis put it. Sometimes it seems as if there is no goodness or beauty left. Creation suffers under the curse, and sinful humanity has raped the earth in tragic ways. We know that one day a "new heaven and a new earth" will blossom forth, but, just as we refuse to resign ourselves to the sin that is destroying our lives, so we refuse to resign ourselves to the evil that is destroying creation.

Were it not for the fall, Luther says, "every tree and branch would have been more esteemed than if it were gold or silver. And properly considered every green tree is lovelier than gold and silver."[6] Perhaps this is where we begin—by recovering a deeper appreciation of nature. Let us see every tree, every leaf, every blade of grass as the loving creation of God's hand, infused with his life and echoing his praise. Let us delight in protecting and caring for our Father's world.

Questions of Examen and Exercises of Devotion

1. In what specific aspect of God's creation is his hand most evident to me? What part do I enjoy the most?
2. Do I have any attitudes or habits that dishonor or desecrate God's creation?
3. Sing this song as you take a walk. Enjoy the Father's world, and let him speak to you everywhere.
4. Consider what work you can do on behalf of the creation, for example, join an environmental organization, or promote local laws that preserve and care for the earth.

The Prayer of the Heart

Father, forgive my careless greed, which contributes to the destruction of your world. Forgive my blindness and deafness to the wonders of nature through which you constantly speak. Help me hear and join in the praises of creation. Help me care for and esteem all that you have made. Amen.

Ubi Caritas

(Where There Is Charity)

10th Century Latin Hymn

Jacques Berthier

U - bi ca - ri - tas_____ et a - mor,_____

U - bi ca - ri - tas_____ De - us i - bi est.

Scripture Reading:
John 13:31–35, 15:12–17, 17:20–26

In these Scriptures Jesus is speaking to his disciples during their final gathering, their last meal together before his death. He has just washed their feet, and they have witnessed the defection of one among them. Notice that in the first two passages Jesus is addressing the disciples. In the last passage he speaks to his Father on their behalf as well as for "those who will believe in me through their word"—for all Christians everywhere.

Scripture Meditation: John 13:34 (RSV)

A new commandment I give to you, that you love one another; even as I have loved you, that you also love one another.

"Love one another." It is often one of the first Bible verses a child learns. Jesus teaches it here to his own "little children" (v. 33). Place yourself among them. Memorize his words. Meditate upon them. Call to mind all of the ways Jesus has loved you: generously, patiently, forgivingly, sacrificially, unconditionally, unceasingly. Now, reflect on your own love for your sisters and brothers in Christ.

Reflecting in Song

The hymn *Ubi Caritas* is a tenth-century Latin hymn of unknown origin. It is traditionally a part of the Mass for Maundy Thursday in the Roman Catholic Church. On Maundy Thursday, the eve of Jesus' crucifixion, two events are commemorated: the Lord's Supper, and the washing of the disciples' feet. The rite of foot washing is known as the Mandatum, or the Maundy, taken from the Latin text of John 13:34: "*Mandatum novum do nobis*"—"a new *commandment* I give you." Washing one another's feet is the practical outworking of this new commandment to "love one another." In the Mass *Ubi Caritas* is sung during the foot washing in preparation for the Holy Communion.

This musical setting, which uses the opening sentence of the hymn, is from the Taizé Community.[7] The community at Taizé finds that the use of Latin is helpful and unifying for those who come there from around the world. Latin is a singable language with a long history of use among Christians, and since it is no longer anyone's native tongue, all can approach it equally. Familiarize yourself with the Latin and sing through the song several times.[8]

Now, meditate upon *Ubi Caritas*. The entire hymn is very long, but the three verses commonly used are given below. Begin by singing this song. You may want to memorize it. As you meditate, pause to sing the song in response as indicated (R).

Where there is charity and love, God is there.
The love of Christ has gathered us together.
Let us rejoice and be glad in it.
Let us revere and love the living God.
And from a sincere heart let us love one another. (R)

Where there is charity and love, God is there.
Likewise, therefore, when we come together let us be
    united as one;
Let us be careful, lest we be divided in intention.
Let us cease all quarrels and strife.
And let Christ dwell in the midst of us. (R)

Where there is charity and love, God is there.
May we also see, along with the blessed,
The glory of your face, O Christ.
And let there be immeasurable joy
Both now and forever more. Amen. (R)

Jesus says the world will know whether or not we are Christians not by our doctrine or our words but by our visible love for one another (John 13:35). Even more sobering, it is by this visible love that the world will know that the Father has sent the Son, that Jesus is the Christ (John 17:23). This kind of love is found in humble acts of service, in washing one another's feet. "Little children, let us not love in word or speech but in deed and truth" (1 John 3:18, RSV).

Questions of Examen and Exercises of Devotion

1. Is there someone in the body of Christ of whom I need to ask forgiveness? Someone I need to forgive?
2. Is there someone in the body of Christ whose feet I might wash today? Someone I might serve?
3. Have a foot washing as part of a worship service or small group. Read and sing responsively *Ubi Caritas*.
4. For one month begin each day with this prayer: "Today, Lord, lead me to someone I can serve."

The Prayer of the Heart

In the name of Jesus and for the sake of Jesus increase charity and love within me today. Amen.

In Christ There Is No East or West

ST. PETER (C.M.)

John Oxenham, 1908, alt.

Alexander R. Reinagle, c. 1830

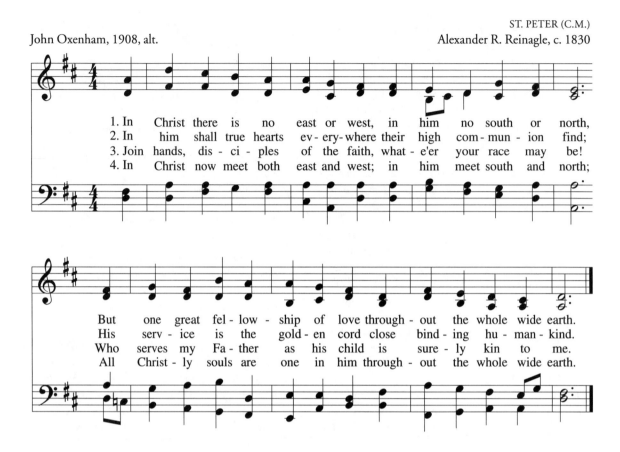

1. In Christ there is no east or west, in him no south or north,
2. In him shall true hearts ev-ery-where their high com-mun-ion find;
3. Join hands, dis-ci-ples of the faith, what-e'er your race may be!
4. In Christ now meet both east and west; in him meet south and north;

But one great fel-low-ship of love through-out the whole wide earth.
His serv-ice is the gold-en cord close bind-ing hu-man-kind.
Who serves my Fa-ther as his child is sure-ly kin to me.
All Christ-ly souls are one in him through-out the whole wide earth.

Scripture Reading: Galatians 3:19–29

The Galatians were Gentile converts to the Christian faith. Paul writes here to warn them of the Judaizers, Jewish Christians who were teaching that Gentiles must submit to the Jewish law in order to be saved. Notice how Paul describes the role of the law and how justification by faith in Christ supersedes that law.

Scripture Meditation: Galatians 3:27–28

As many of you as were baptized into Christ have clothed yourselves with Christ. There is no longer Jew or Greek, there is no longer slave or free, there is no longer male and female; for all of you are one in Christ Jesus.

As you reflect on this verse, call to mind your own baptism. Picture yourself "clothed with Christ," covered with his strength and love and completely identified with him. See your brothers and sisters in Christ throughout the world in the same way. Realize that in your identification with Christ you identify with all who belong to him.

Reflecting in Song

"For Christians are not differentiated from other people by country, language, or customs. . . . They live in both Greek and foreign cities [and] follow local customs in clothing, food and the other aspects of life. But at the same time, they demonstrate to us the wonderful and certainly unusual form of their own citizenship. They live in their own native lands, but as aliens; as citizens, they share all things with others; but like aliens, suffer all things. Every foreign country is to them as their native country, and every native land as a foreign country."[9] So did an anonymous observer describe Christians of the second century—a community without geographic or national boundaries. Sing this hymn, which is a twentieth-century description of that same community: "one great fellowship of love throughout the whole wide earth."

The body of Christ is international, and it is also interdependent. This "fellowship of love" is a fellowship based upon serving, sharing, suffering with one another, for "if one member suffers, all suffer together" (1 Cor. 12:26). This is the *koinonia* of the New Testament. It is not just a feeling of community; it is participation and action. The word *koinonia,* which means close fellowship and communion, is also used in reference to monetary gifts made to other Christians (Rom. 15:26; Phil. 4:15). Believers have a mandate to "work for the good of all, and *especially* for those of the family of faith" (Gal. 6:10, italics added). Recently an African Christian expressed his extreme gratitude to an American Christian, a doctor who had chosen to return to Zaire at great personal risk following an evacuation due to civil war. "You don't understand how scared we get when you people leave," he said. "We know our lives will never change much, but as long as you're here to provide some stability, we have hope that our children will have it better."[10] Relieving fear, giving hope—this is what "bearing one another's burdens" is all about. Sing the hymn again, and think of your suffering brothers and sisters throughout the world.

The body of Christ is a family, a family that transcends human barriers such as race, nationality, culture, social class, gender, wealth, education, politics, denomination. In Christ all are equal, and all are one. Dietrich Bonhoeffer writes, "Without Christ we should not know God, we could not call upon Him, nor come to Him. But without Christ we also would not know our brother, nor could we come to him. The way is blocked by our own ego. Christ opened up the way to God and to our brother. Now Christians can live with one another in peace; they can love and serve one another; they can become one. But they can continue to do so only by way of Jesus Christ. Only in Jesus Christ are we one, only through him are we bound together. To eternity he remains the one Mediator."[11] Sing the hymn one more time, and give thanks for the unity we share with one another because of Christ.

Questions of Examen and Exercises of Devotion

1. Which human barriers are hardest for me personally to transcend (social, racial, sexual, and so forth)? Do I give preference to certain types of Christians? Do I prejudge certain types?
2. What might I do this week to overcome one of my prejudgments?
3. Continue this list: "In Christ there is neither Jew nor Greek, male nor female, blue collar nor white collar, Democrat nor Republican, charismatic nor fundamentalist. . . ."
4. Find out more about suffering Christians in another part of the world. Make them a special focus for prayer, help, and financial support.

The Prayer of the Heart

Thank you, Lord, for the whole family. I am so glad that I am not alone, that I am a part of peoples from every race and nation and tribe and tongue on earth. Thank you, thank you for gathering such an all-inclusive community of loving persons. And thank you for being at the heart of this community as its sustainer and most glorious inhabitant. I speak this thanksgiving prayer in Jesus' name. Amen.

Here I Am, Lord

Daniel L. Schutte

Daniel L. Schutte

Not too fast

1. I, the Lord of sea and sky, I have heard my peo - ple cry.
2. I, the Lord of snow and rain, I have borne my peo - ple's pain.
3. I, the Lord of wind and flame, I will tend the poor and lame,

All who dwell in dark and sin my hand will save. I who made the
I have wept for love of them. They turn a - way. I will break their
I will set a feast for them. My hand will save. Fin - est bread I

stars of night, I will make their dark - ness bright. Who will bear my
hearts of stone, give them hearts for love a - lone. I will speak my
will pro - vide till their hearts be sat - is - fied. I will give my

light to them? Whom shall I send?
word to them. Whom shall I send?
life to them. Whom shall I send?

Refrain

Here I am, Lord. Is it

I, Lord? I have heard you call - ing in the night. I will go, Lord,

if you lead me. I will hold your peo - ple in my heart.

© 1981, Daniel L. Schutte and New Dawn Music

Songs of Shalom

Scripture Reading: 1 Samuel 3, Isaiah 6

These chapters recount the call and commissioning of two great prophets of Israel. See how each placed himself before God prior to hearing God's call. Isaiah sees a glorious vision of God in his holiness; Samuel ministers to God, spends time in God's presence, and even sleeps near the ark. Note their responses to God and the message each is given to deliver.

Scripture Meditation: Isaiah 6:8

> Then I heard the voice of the Lord saying, "Whom shall I send, and who will go for us?" And I said, "Here am I; send me!"

Meditate upon this passage, God's call to Isaiah. Now, do as Isaiah and Samuel did, and place yourself before God in "holy expectancy." Quietly spend time in praise and adoration, confessing any sin that comes to mind. In the words of Samuel, invite God to "speak, for your servant is listening." Be attentive for his voice.

Reflecting in Song

What matters to God is not our ability but our availability. This song concerns our availability—allowing ourselves to be used by God, no matter where he calls us. Read it and notice the dialogue: God calls, we respond. Sing the first verse of the song.

One who made himself unconditionally available to God was Dr. Paul Carlson, medical missionary to the Congo (now Zaire) in the early 1960s.[12] He, with his family, went to the remote village of Wasolo, so obscure it was known as "*le coin perdu*"—"the lost corner"—where he served an area that had no other physician. In 1964 a military uprising occurred and many Christians were murdered. Most Americans evacuated, but Paul, in spite of the danger, stayed behind to treat his patients. In November of 1964 Paul Carlson was gunned down by rebel soldiers. As you sing the second verse, think of the sacrifice of this present-day martyr who gave his life so that others could live.

For nearly twenty years following Paul's death the Wasolo hospital was not permanently staffed. But in the early 1980s Dr. Dean Samuelson, having completed his training at Harvard Medical School, became aware of the tremendous need at Wasolo. He and his wife, Gretchen, decided to respond with a long-term commitment. Taking their four (now six) children, they moved to Wasolo, where Dean is often the only physician for approximately two hundred thousand people scattered throughout an area the size of Iowa. It is an area of abject poverty where a person might own nothing but a machete, a cooking pot, and the clothes on his or her back. Medicines are scarce and equipment is primitive, but every day someone lives who would have died had the Samuelsons not made themselves available. Sing the third verse. Think of the "poor and lame" of the world who are still waiting for help.

Life for any missionary is challenging and sacrificial. The Samuelsons live in a remote, isolated jungle with no phone, no television, unreliable water, and sporadic electricity. There are no grocery stores, shopping malls, or restaurants. In addition to the poverty and disease, they fight a constant battle with witchcraft, idol worship, and spiritism and face the continuing threat of civil war. Yet they witness to the incomparable blessing, the joy, the peace in "knowing that every day you're saving lives, and you're exactly where God wants you to be."[13]

Consider where God is calling you today. Give him your fears, hesitations, and objections, whether large or small. Ask where you are needed to bring life and health, wholeness and peace into God's hurting world. It may be in Africa, or it may be across the street. Sing the entire song once again. Make yourself available.

Questions of Examen and Exercises of Devotion

1. In what ways have I made myself available to God this past week?
2. Often it is the little things that hinder our availability. Gretchen Samuelson admits that chocolate ice cream almost kept her from going to Africa. Are there little things hindering my availability? Big things?
3. Write down three things you can do to make yourself more available to answer God's call.
4. For seven days straight take five minutes to listen for God's call. Watch for course corrections that are ever so slight.

The Prayer of the Heart

What does it mean to be available to you, Lord, in the midst of so much pain and suffering in the world? I simply cannot respond to every need, but perhaps there is one thing I can do. If so, show me what it is, and then help me to do that one thing with all my might. Amen.

Songs of the Word

Our message is Jesus Christ; we dare not give less,
and we cannot give more.

—*William Temple*

We are sustained by every word that proceeds from the mouth of God; we
feast on Christ, the living Word of God; and we are informed and formed
by the Scriptures, the written Word of God.

Having once tasted of God's life and truth, it would be wrong of us to
withhold what we have been given. Freely we have received, freely we give.
Richard Baxter, the influential Puritan leader, declared:

> *I preached, as never sure to preach again*
> *And as a dying man to dying men.*

All of this is done with the deepest humility of heart. We can get some
things wrong—and probably do. The fact that God speaks to us is no guarantee that we hear correctly. The fact that Jesus is the Way, the Truth, and
the Life is no guarantee that we present him free of our own cultural accou-
trements. The facts of the Scripture can often be twisted to serve our own
ends. And so, even as we share our faith—perhaps especially as we share
our faith—we are always teachable, always learning, always growing.

Our Father

Miriam Overholt

Miriam Overholt

Freely, as a chant

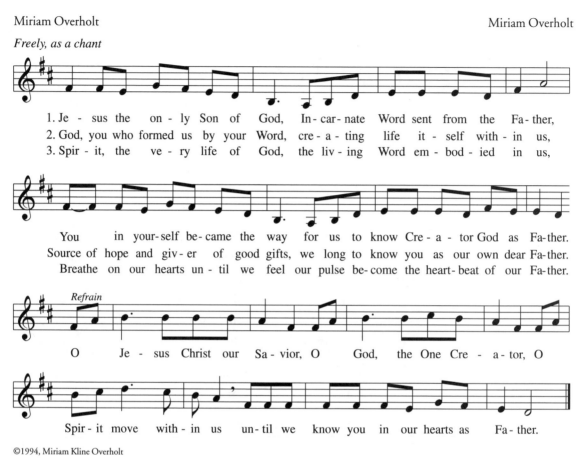

1. Je - sus the on - ly Son of God, In - car - nate Word sent from the Fa - ther,
2. God, you who formed us by your Word, cre - a - ting life it - self with - in us,
3. Spir - it, the ve - ry life of God, the liv - ing Word em - bod - ied in us,

You in your-self be - came the way for us to know Cre - a - tor God as Fa-ther.
Source of hope and giv - er of good gifts, we long to know you as our own dear Fa-ther.
Breathe on our hearts un - til we feel our pulse be - come the heart-beat of our Fa-ther.

Refrain

O Je - sus Christ our Sa - vior, O God, the One Cre - a-tor, O

Spir - it move with - in us un - til we know you in our hearts as Fa - ther.

Accompaniment for this song is found on page 144.

Scripture Reading: John 1:1–18

Notice how the Gospel of John opens with the same words as the book of Genesis: "In the beginning . . ." In this way John identifies the Word with God himself, preexistent to and active in the creation of all things. But not until verse 14 do we realize the full impact of John's message: "The Word became flesh." God became human! And this incarnate Word is none other than Jesus Christ.

Scripture Meditation: John 1:14 (RSV)

And the Word became flesh and dwelt among us,
full of grace and truth; we have beheld his glory, glory
as of the only Son from the Father.

As you meditate on these words, imagine you are hear-ing them for the first time: "The Word became flesh and dwelt among us." Ponder the astounding reality of the incarnation. Give thanks to God for his Word made flesh. Now, look at the phrase "full of grace and truth." The living Word is God's communication of both his grace—his mercy, forgiveness, and love—and his truth, the truth about God and about ourselves. In Jesus we see both of these, grace and truth, fully embodied and perfectly balanced. "And from his fullness have we *all* received, grace upon grace" (v. 16).

Reflecting in Song

This song of the incarnate Word is a prayer—a prayer that we might know God deeply, personally, and intimately as our Father. Read through it and notice that each verse addresses a different Person of the Trinity, while the refrain addresses all three. See how the Word is expressed through each Person.

The music of this song is chantlike, with a free rhythmic structure. It should be sung smoothly and freely, giving emphasis to the main words in each phrase, rather than with a strict beat. Now, sing the song.

Composer and author Miriam Overholt tells how this song originated during a retreat she and her husband attended in 1982: "We were asked to spend a day and night in silence. This was a new experience for me, and at first I rebelled in my spirit. Being an overachiever, it was difficult to be still or silent. But finally I gave in and tried to be quiet. During the afternoon I felt drawn to an open field and sat down in the sun on a big rock. I struggled with inadequacy, but being quiet took away most of my ammunition to use in proving myself to God. During that afternoon of silence God told me to rest and enjoy just being quiet in His presence. I slept and woke and prayed, and the sunlight was a warm, comforting representation of God's closeness and acceptance. Later that day, I wrote this song.

"God assured me in the depths of my heart that day that He is my loving, affirming Father. Of course I forget very often and try to prove myself to Him again. But through the work of Jesus Christ on the cross, we are assured of God's outgoing love for us. And as we invite Him to work in us, God's Spirit breathes on our hearts and convinces us of our place in God."

Some, having known only hurt and abuse at the hands of their earthly fathers, struggle to relate to God as Father. A friend, Tina, is one of these. But over a period of years God's gracious Spirit has been breathing on her heart, and she witnesses how "Father is revealing himself to me in new ways all the time. He really is becoming the Father I always wanted but never had."

Perhaps you had a loving, caring earthly father. If so, give thanks and realize that God's great love far exceeds that of even the best earthly father. Perhaps you have suffered deeply from abuse or neglect by your human father. If so, allow God's healing touch to replace this ugly, distorted picture of fatherhood for you. Accept God's grace and mercy. See how good it is to be Abba's child. Allow yourself to be embraced by the Abba heart of God. Now, sing this song again.

Questions of Examen and Exercises of Devotion

1. Am I fearful of the Father heart of God?
2. This song sets forth God as the Creative Word, Christ as the Incarnate Word, and the Spirit as the Living Word. How do I experience this "word" characteristic of God?
3. Spend a complete day in silence.
4. Notice that this song begins with Jesus and bridges from Jesus to God. The theological basis for this is the Christlikeness of God; that is, we understand what God is like by looking at the revelation given to us in Jesus Christ. This being the case, from your study of the Gospels, write out a list of the attributes of Jesus and see what that teaches you about the character of God.

The Prayer of the Heart

O Lord, I shrink back from the smoke of Sinai and the flames of Carmel. But as your Son, Jesus, opens to me your Abba heart, I feel your welcome. And so I come, I come. Amen.

All Hail the Power of Jesus' Name

CORONATION (C.M. with repeats)

Edward Perronet, 1779; alt. by John Rippon, 1787

Oliver Holden, 1793

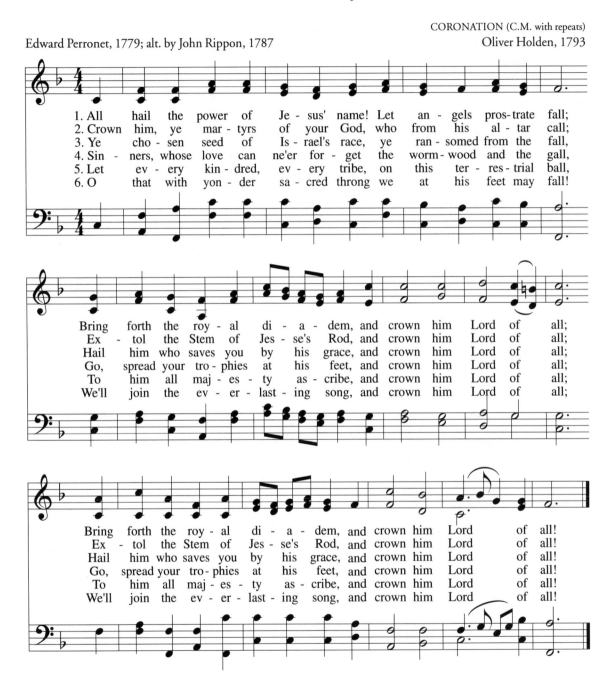

1. All hail the power of Je - sus' name! Let an - gels pros-trate fall;
2. Crown him, ye mar - tyrs of your God, who from his al - tar call;
3. Ye cho - sen seed of Is - rael's race, ye ran - somed from the fall,
4. Sin - ners, whose love can ne'er for - get the worm - wood and the gall,
5. Let ev - ery kin - dred, ev - ery tribe, on this ter - res - trial ball,
6. O that with yon - der sa - cred throng we at his feet may fall!

Bring forth the roy - al di - a - dem, and crown him Lord of all;
Ex - tol the Stem of Jes - se's Rod, and crown him Lord of all;
Hail him who saves you by his grace, and crown him Lord of all;
Go, spread your tro - phies at his feet, and crown him Lord of all;
To him all maj - es - ty as - cribe, and crown him Lord of all;
We'll join the ev - er - last - ing song, and crown him Lord of all;

Bring forth the roy - al di - a - dem, and crown him Lord of all!
Ex - tol the Stem of Jes - se's Rod, and crown him Lord of all!
Hail him who saves you by his grace, and crown him Lord of all!
Go, spread your tro - phies at his feet, and crown him Lord of all!
To him all maj - es - ty as - cribe, and crown him Lord of all!
We'll join the ev - er - last - ing song, and crown him Lord of all!

Scripture Reading: Philippians 2:6–11

This passage is generally thought to be an early hymn of the Church. "Every knee shall bow, every tongue shall swear" is taken from Isaiah 45:23 and used here in reference to Christ. Notice how the first three verses focus on the humiliation of Christ, the last three on his exaltation.

Scripture Meditation: Philippians 2:9–11 (RSV)

Therefore God has highly exalted him and bestowed on him the name which is above every name, that at the name of Jesus every knee should bow, in heaven and on earth and under the earth, and every tongue confess that Jesus Christ is Lord, to the glory of God the Father.

"Jesus is Lord!" It was one of the earliest creeds of the Christian church. It is the essence of this Scripture passage. As you memorize this Scripture, join in this ancient confession, "Jesus is Lord." Sing the song in proclamation of his Lordship.

Reflecting in Song

The greatest source of power on earth remains the most untapped. It is the all-powerful name of Jesus. If we could truly realize and use but a fraction of this power in our day-to-day living, what a difference it would make not only in our lives but in the Church, in society, and in the world!

In the name of Jesus, and only in the name of Jesus, is the power of salvation, "for there is no other name under heaven given among mortals by which we must be saved" (Acts 4:12). In Jesus' name we can do the works that he does and even "greater works than these, because I am going to the Father. I will do whatever you ask in my name, so that the Father may be glorified in the Son" (John 14:12–13). *Anything* we ask, for the sake of his name and the glory of God, Jesus will do! In his name are also strength and protection: "The name of the LORD is a strong tower; the righteous run into it and are safe" (Prov. 18:10). And Jesus' name means ultimate victory, for he is "far above all rule and authority and power and dominion, and above every name that is named, not only in this age but also in the age to come" (Eph. 1:21).

So often we fight a losing battle because we do not recognize just who the enemy is. We use the wrong weapons, forgetting that we are battling "the cosmic powers of this present darkness" (Eph. 6:12). This hymn serves as a reminder of the only effective power for our battle. It is also a means of exercising that power. When we praise the name of Jesus, the enemy flees. As Charles Wesley wrote:

Jesus! the name high over all, In hell, or earth, or sky; Angels and men before it fall, And devils fear and fly.[1]

Sing "All Hail the Power of Jesus' Name" again, realizing that in your singing "devils fear and fly."

Edward Perronet, the author of this hymn, was a friend of Charles and John Wesley. During 1749 he traveled with John as an itinerant preacher. Many times they would be met by angry mobs. John records one occasion when stones were hurled at them and "Edward Perronet was thrown down and rolled in mud and mire."[2] Nevertheless, Perronet continued to preach, and he wrote several volumes of hymns. This is the only one that has endured. But what a legacy this single hymn has been! Translated into countless languages, it continues to be sung throughout "this terrestrial ball."

The hymn is sung to several different tunes. This tune, CORONATION, was written by Oliver Holden, a carpenter from Massachusetts. It is especially appropriate to the majestic nature of the text. As you sing the hymn once again, picture yourself joining with all those mentioned here—angels and martyrs, saints and sinners, every kindred, every tribe. Worship Jesus. Hail the power of his almighty, eternal name. Crown him Lord of all!

Questions of Examen and Exercises of Devotion

1. Do I treat the name of Jesus glibly or with an inner spirit of prostration?
2. In what way have I experienced something of the power of Jesus' name recently?
3. Begin your day with a housecleaning. Sing this song before you start your work. Make the devils fear and fly!
4. As you do your work this next week, see what attitudes you might have and actions you might do that honor Jesus and "crown him Lord of all."

The Prayer of the Heart

I would like to live this day with you, Jesus. I'm not thinking about tomorrow or the years ahead, only today. Can I live this solitary day with you as the Lord of all—Lord over my thoughts and feelings and attitudes and actions? I would like that. Amen, may it be so.

I Will Change Your Name

D. J. Butler

D. J. Butler

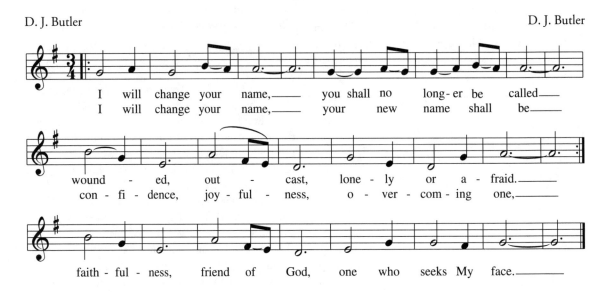

I will change your name,
You shall no longer be called
    wounded, outcast, lonely or afraid.

I will change your name,
Your new name shall be
    confidence, joyfulness, overcoming one,
    faithfulness, friend of God, one who seeks My face.

Accompaniment for this song is found on page 146.

Scripture Reading: Isaiah 62:1–5, 11–12

In this Scripture the victory, salvation, and glory of Jerusalem—the city of God—shine forth for all to see. The people of God are likened to a beautiful, beloved bride. As a prophecy this passage applies not only to the Jerusalem of Isaiah's day but also to the Jerusalem above, the Church universal, which is the bride of Christ (Gal. 4:24–27). Note what delight and enjoyment God takes in his bride, and the many new names he gives to her (vv. 3, 4, 12).

Scripture Meditation: Isaiah 62:2b–3

You shall be called by a new name
   that the mouth of the LORD will give.
You shall be a crown of beauty in the hand of the
   LORD,
   and a royal diadem in the hand of your God.

Contemplate this promise of God. Let it speak to you personally, inserting your own name after each *you*. Consider the tremendous worth of a "crown of beauty," a "royal diadem"—in the hand of the Lord, no less. Know how very precious you are to God. Now, sing this song.

Reflecting in Song

"There's a new name written down in glory, and it's mine, oh yes, it's mine," says an old gospel song, as the angels rejoice that "a sinner has come home." And indeed, Scripture tells us that believers' names are recorded in the "book of life" (Phil. 4:3, Rev. 21:27) and that God has a "new name" for each of us (Rev. 2:17).

We tend to think of this new name as something we will receive later—in the perfection of heaven, perhaps. After all, what does it matter for our lives now? What's in a name, anyway? The answer is: everything. Identity. Self-worth. Names *do* matter. "Sticks and stones will break my bones, but words will break my heart."[3] Or, heal it. The names we call ourselves, the names we are called especially by our loved ones, the names we call others—all have the power to make or break lives. Reflect on the names you are called and on the names, both positive and negative, that you call others. Sing the song again.

Shortly after our (Janet's) daughter was born, Ken took her in his arms and named her "my Darling Precious Angel Princess." It was a name too long for the birth certificate, so we settled for "Annie." But the appellation has remained—her own, special name from her father.

Much more than any earthly father cherishes his precious child, so does God cherish you. And just as the love of a mother cannot be exhausted no matter how many children she may have, so God's love is inexhaustible. "Can a woman forget her nursing child, or show no compassion for the child of her womb? Even these may forget, yet I will not forget you. See, I have inscribed you on the palms of my hands" (Isa. 49:15–16).

Think of it—God has his own, special name for you, the apple of his eye. He to whom time is no barrier chose you before the foundation of the world, formed you in the womb, and knows and calls you by your new name right now. Sing this song once again and hear God speaking these words to you. Listen in quietness. Accept and affirm the names that he gives. Ask God to help you live in the identity and the reality of your new name.

Questions of Examen and Exercises of Devotion

1. Are there any particular names from which you need healing and freedom? Let God's Spirit use this song to help you.
2. Do you know one who is "wounded, outcast, lonely, or afraid"? Pray this song into his or her life.
3. Memorize these names: "Confidence, Joyfulness, Overcoming one; Faithfulness, Friend of God, One who seeks my face." Write them down, and put them where you will see them often. Find Scriptures to support each one. For example, on Confidence: "I can do all things through him who strengthens me" (Phil. 4:13).
4. In your Bible reading ask the Holy Spirit to show you other new names—new identities—that God gives you in Christ.

The Prayer of the Heart

Dearest Jesus, sometimes I feel defined by those aspects of me that feel weak and vulnerable. Speak the word, Lord, that will redefine me. Amen.

Shine, Jesus, Shine

Graham Kendrick   Graham Kendrick

1. Lord, the light of your love is shin-ing in the midst of the dark-ness, shin-ing; Je-sus, Light of the World, shine up-on us, set us free by the truth you now bring us: Shine on me, Shine on me.

Refrain

Shine, Je-sus, shine, fill this land with the Fa-ther's glo-ry, Blaze, Spir-it, blaze, set our hearts on fire. Flow, riv-er, flow, flood the na-tions with grace and mer-cy, Send forth your word, Lord, and let there be light!

2. Lord, I come to your awesome presence,
From the shadows into your radiance;
By the blood I may enter your brightness,
Search me, try me, consume all my darkness:
Shine on me, shine on me.

3. As we gaze on your kingly brightness,
So our faces display your likeness,
Ever changing from glory to glory,
Mirrored here may our lives tell your story:
Shine on me, shine on me.

Accompaniment for this song is found on page 148.

Scripture Reading: Isaiah 9:2–7, John 8:12

The passage in Isaiah carries a promise of the coming Messiah—One who will bring light and joy, freedom and peace while ruling with authority, justice, and righteousness. Reflect on how Jesus has fulfilled these prophecies and how they will be even further realized when he reigns in glory. Notice how Jesus' own words understood in the light of Isaiah's prophecy witness to the fact that he is, indeed, the promised Messiah.

Scripture Meditation: Isaiah 9:2, John 8:12

The people who walked in darkness have seen a great light; those who lived in a land of deep darkness— on them has light shined.

Again Jesus spoke to them saying, "I am the light of the world. Whoever follows me will never walk in darkness but will have the light of life."

Memorize these Scriptures if possible. Consider them as the Israel of Isaiah's day and then of Jesus' day might have heard them. Think of them as they apply to your world and your culture. Recall dark days in your past into which Jesus has shed his light. Take heart in his words.

Reflecting in Song

"Moment by moment it seems like the world just slips into another shade of darkness without You." So sings Annie Herring.[4] And we can identify. Despite material prosperity ours is a time of spiritual poverty evidenced by growing crime, violence, and disregard for human life. We fear for our safety and the safety of our children. Even more, we fear for the spiritual lives of our children as we witness the moral decay of contemporary culture. It seems that what is good and true and beautiful is all but banished from the public square.

We are not the first to live in times of increasing darkness, as the Scriptures remind us. This song is an affirmation of the light that shines in the darkness and that the darkness has not, cannot, and will not overcome (John 1:5). Graham Kendrick, a London minister, wrote "Shine, Jesus, Shine" in 1988. It was born out of his longing for global spiritual awakening. Closely associated with the March for Jesus movement, the song has already become known around the world.

Jesus Christ, the light of the world, is the only hope for the world, the only light in the darkness. And we,

his body, are his means of bringing that light. "You are the light of the world," he says (Matt. 5:14). But in order to bring light we must be people of the light. Only as we allow Jesus to shine his light into every corner of our lives—our hearts, our homes, our friendships, our work, our churches—will we be pure and clear and clean. Only then can his light shine out for all to see. Notice how the verses of this song focus on Christ's light within, asking that it "shine on me," after which the refrain asks that his light shine out into the world. Pray through each of these verses. Then sing the song.

Darkness is forbidding because it instills fear—fear of the unknown and unseen. Spiritual darkness is real, and it is evil. But the light of Christ always prevails; no darkness is powerful enough to extinguish it. So as you look around and see the darkness encroaching, do not be afraid. For as veteran journalist Malcolm Muggeridge has said, "It is precisely when every earthly hope has been explored and found wanting, . . . when every recourse this world offers, moral as well as material, has been explored to no effect, when in the shivering cold the last stick of wood has been thrown on the fire and in the gathering darkness every glimmer of light has finally flickered out—it is then that Christ's hand reaches out, sure and firm, that Christ's words bring their inexpressible comfort, that his light shines brightest, abolishing the darkness forever."[5] Shine, Jesus, shine!

Questions of Examen and Exercises of Devotion

1. What areas of darkness am I personally experiencing today?
2. What areas of darkness in society am I currently battling?
3. As you encounter pockets of darkness in your world, speak forth: "Shine, Jesus, shine into this (street, school, business, political entity, newspaper)."
4. Make a concerted prayer effort during the coming week for an individual in whom you sense a need for the light of life. Ask Christ to shine his light into him or her.

The Prayer of the Heart

Lord, thank you that the light of your love shines in the midst of our darkness. Shine on me. Shine into me. Shine through me. Flood the nations with your glory. Send forth your word. Let there be light! Amen.

O for a Thousand Tongues to Sing

AZMON (C.M.)
Charles Wesley, 1739
Carl G. Gläser, 1828

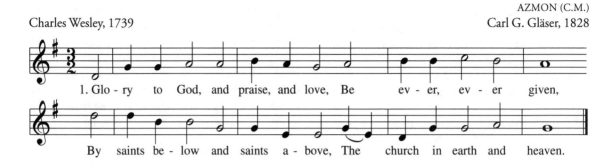

1. Glo-ry to God, and praise, and love, Be ev-er, ev-er given,
By saints be-low and saints a-bove, The church in earth and heaven.

2. On this glad day the glorious Sun
Of Righteousness arose;
On my benighted soul He shone,
And filled it with repose.

3. Sudden expired the legal strife;
'Twas then I ceased to grieve;
My second, real, living life
I then began to live.

4. Then with my heart I first believed,
Believed with faith Divine;
Power with the Holy Ghost received
To call the Savior mine.

5. I felt my Lord's atoning blood
Close to my soul applied,
Me, me He loved—the Son of God,
For me, for me He died!

6. O for a thousand tongues to sing
My dear Redeemer's praise!
The glories of my God and King,
The triumphs of His grace.

7. My gracious Master, and my God,
Assist me to proclaim,
To spread through all the earth abroad
The honours of Thy name.

8. Jesus, the name that charms our fears,
That bids our sorrows cease;
'Tis music in the sinner's ears,
'Tis life, and health, and peace!

9. He breaks the power of cancelled sin,
He sets the prisoner free;
His blood can make the foulest clean,
His blood availed for me.

10. He speaks; and, listening to His voice,
New life the dead receive,
The mournful, broken hearts rejoice,
The humble poor believe.

11. Hear Him, ye deaf; His praise, ye dumb,
Your loosened tongues employ;
Ye blind, behold your Saviour come;
And leap, ye lame, for joy.

12. Look unto Him, ye nations; own
Your God, ye fallen race!
Look, and be saved through faith alone;
Be justified by grace!

13. See all your sins on Jesus laid;
The Lamb of God was slain,
His soul was once an offering made
For every soul of man.

14. Harlots, and publicans, and thieves
In holy triumph join;
Saved is the sinner that believes
From crimes as great as mine.

15. With me, your chief, you then shall know,
Shall feel your sins forgiven;
Anticipate your heaven below,
And own that love is heaven.

Scripture Reading: Psalm 40:1–10

In the first five verses of this passage the psalmist tells of the deliverance of God, joyfully singing and proclaiming God's faithfulness. The next five verses describe the grateful response of one so blessed: an ear ready to hear God's voice, a will delighting to obey, a heart attuned to God's law, and a mouth eager to speak forth the "glad news of deliverance."

Scripture Meditation: Psalm 40:3

> *He put a new song in my mouth, a song of praise to our God.*
> *Many will see and fear, and put their trust in the LORD.*

Repeat this verse several times until it flows. Notice its natural rhythm, which makes it easy to memorize. Consider this "new song" of deliverance—how it is not something we make up but something that is given by God himself. Clement of Alexandria referred to Christ as the "New Song." Reflect on the verse in that context. Finally, note how this God-given new song is used to draw others to Him.

Reflecting in Song

Charles Wesley, author of this hymn, was converted on Pentecost Sunday in 1738, three days prior to his brother John's famed Aldersgate experience where he felt his "heart strangely warmed." As Charles read from his Bible on that Sunday, this verse from Psalm 40, along with verses from Isaiah 40 ("Comfort, comfort ye my people") spoke directly to him. Charles could finally believe his sins were forgiven and that salvation did not depend upon his own works but on the merits of Christ. He wrote, "I now found myself at peace with God, and rejoiced in the hope of loving Christ."[6] One year later in commemoration of the event, he wrote this hymn. Read through these original stanzas and see how Charles Wesley describes his experience of forgiveness. Now, sing the hymn in its more common, shorter form—verses six through eleven.[7]

Prior to his conversion Charles had written hymns, but now, with God's new song in his heart, the hymns poured forth freely. Everywhere he went, traveling and preaching with John, he wrote hymns—over sixty-five hundred in all.[8] An associate of the Wesleys recalled how Charles would ride on horseback and enter their home calling, "Pen and ink! Pen and ink!" After writing out his latest hymn, he would then greet his hosts.[9]

While John shaped the theology of the Methodists, Charles sang it into their hearts with his hymns. Like Martin Luther before him and Fanny Crosby after him, he wrote for the masses—or, in his case, the "unruly mob" that was often the Wesleys' congregation. Charles introduced a new kind of hymnody in England—hymns of Christian experience and evangelical emphasis. He used new meters and tunes and drew from secular songs, popular songs, even coarse drinking songs, which he "converted" for his use, believing that:

> *Listed into the cause of sin, why should a good be evil?*
> *Music, alas, too long has been pressed to obey the devil.*[10]

Charles's hymns were widely sung at informal Methodist gatherings, but during his lifetime they were not sung in worship in his own church, the Church of England.[11] His hymns, along with all "hymns of human composure," were often associated with Christian extremism and sung by those on the periphery of organized religion. Not until 1820, thirty-two years after Charles's death, was the singing of hymns officially approved by the Church of England.

Now, do something radical and sing this hymn once again! Realize how Charles Wesley's desire for "a thousand tongues to sing" is being fulfilled over and over again as millions of tongues have joined—and continue to join—in singing praises to God through his hymns.

Questions of Examen and Exercises of Devotion

1. In verse nine Wesley writes, "He breaks the power of cancelled sin." In my life are there sins that are canceled, that is, forgiven, but that still have power over me? If so, seek Jesus to break their power.
2. Read these fifteen stanzas once again. Relate them to your own experience of forgiveness. Is there one verse with which you can especially identify?
3. Be your own hymn editor. Choose and arrange the stanzas in a way that best speaks to your condition.
4. Make note of and celebrate a spiritual anniversary in your life.

The Prayer of the Heart

A thousand tongues, Lord? I seldom can get one tongue to praise you, let alone a thousand. Now I ask you, if I had a thousand tongues, would they be the cacophony of Babel or the symphony of Pentecost? I wish the latter but fear the former. O Lord, amidst the thousands of robust "Hallelujah's," may my insecure twitter be acceptable in your sight. Amen.

A Mighty Fortress

Martin Luther, ca. 1529 (Ps. 46)
Trans. by Frederick H. Hedge, 1853, alt.

EIN' FESTE BURG (8.7.8.7.6.6.6.6.7.)
Martin Luther, ca. 1529

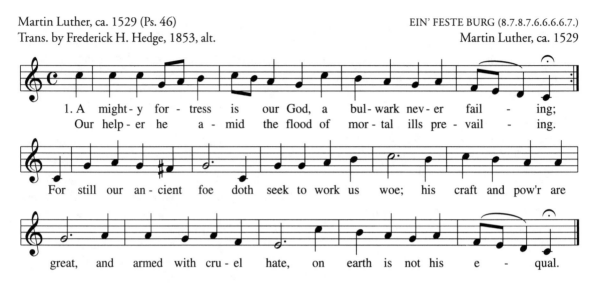

1. A might-y for-tress is our God, a bul-wark nev-er fail - ing;
Our help-er he a-mid the flood of mor-tal ills pre-vail - ing.
For still our an-cient foe doth seek to work us woe; his craft and pow'r are
great, and armed with cru-el hate, on earth is not his e - qual.

2. Did we in our own strength confide, our striving would be losing,
Were not the right man on our side, the man of God's own choosing.
Dost ask who that may be? Christ Jesus, it is he;
Lord Sabaoth his name, from age to age the same.
And he must win the battle.

3. And though this world, with devils filled, should threaten to undo us,
We will not fear, for God hath willed his truth to triumph through us.
The Prince of Darkness grim, we tremble not for him;
His rage we can endure, for lo, his doom is sure.
One little word shall fell him.

4. That Word above all earthly powers, no thanks to them, abideth;
The Spirit and the gifts are ours, through him who with us sideth.
Let goods and kindred go, this mortal life also;
The body they may kill; God's truth abideth still;
The Kingdom's ours forever!

Scripture Reading: Psalm 46

As you read this psalm be aware of its three parts, each marked by a *Selah*. Pause and reflect at each of these "punctuation marks of the Holy Spirit."[12] Notice there is a refrain, verses seven and eleven, which concludes two of the sections.

Scripture Meditation: Psalm 46:1–2, 7 (NIV)

God is our refuge and strength,
an ever-present help in trouble.
Therefore we will not fear, though the earth give
way
and the mountains fall into the heart of the sea . . .

The LORD Almighty is with us;
the God of Jacob is our fortress.

What seems more solid, more enduring, more impregnable than the mountains? People have long sought shelter in mountains—whether of the natural variety or human-made mountains of castles, fortresses, and skyscrapers. Consider how all of these provide no real, lasting security. Contemplate the eternal and ever-present God as your refuge, your strength, your "mighty fortress."

Reflecting in Song

Martin Luther wrote this hymn to apply Psalm 46 to the Church of his day with all of its trials and struggles. The message remains timeless. First, read through the hymn, looking at it from the perspective of a Christian during Luther's day. Now read it again, this time from your own point of view. Does the hymn speak to particular struggles in your life? Now, sing this "Battle Hymn of the Reformation."

This song, with its confident assurance of God's strength, power, and protection, is also a song of spiritual warfare—something Luther felt very keenly. His writings frequently mention personal attacks of Satan, and legend has it that he once hurled an inkwell at the devil. Luther's primary weapon, however, was always the Word of God. To him it was central: "We can spare everything except the Word."[13] Focus on verses three and four, and see what confidence Luther places in the Word of God.

Besides being a pastor, teacher, writer, translator, theologian, and reformer, Luther was also a composer and an accomplished musician. He believed that music was the *viva vox evangelii,* the "living voice of the Gospel," and that "next to the Word of God, music deserves the highest praise."[14] He wrote hymns in the language of the common people so that "the Word of God may be kept alive in them by singing."[15] Note that he wrote both text and melody for this hymn.[16] His tunes were drawn from plainsong, folk songs, and popular music of the day. His hymns spread like wildfire, and Luther's enemies lamented that "the whole people are singing themselves into his doctrines."[17] Under Luther's direction hymns were once again sung in worship by the entire congregation rather than by the clergy alone.

Luther's influence as a reformer is widely recognized, but his contribution to music history is sometimes overlooked. The seventeenth-century shift of musical leadership from Italy to Germany has been credited to the Protestant Reformation, as great composers such as Heinrich Schütz, Johann Pachelbel, and ultimately J. S. Bach emerged in the Lutheran tradition. Luther was immeasurably influential in the life and work of Bach, who not only owned and read Luther's writings but also used Luther's texts and tunes in many of his compositions. This tune, *Ein' feste Burg,* has been used in major works by several composers including Bach, Mendelssohn, and Wagner.

For Luther, singing was a means of instilling the Word of God in human hearts; it was a form of spiritual warfare—"the Devil flies before the sound of music almost as much as before the Word of God"[18]—and it was just plain fun. Luther often sang and played the lute with his family and friends, who commented how "merry in heart" he became when he sang and how he never seemed to tire of it. Sing his hymn once again. Rejoice that "the Lord Almighty is with us; the God of Jacob is our fortress."

Questions of Examen and Exercises of Devotion

1. On what things do I rely for daily strength and protection?
2. How might I rely more on God as my "refuge and strength"?
3. As you encounter temptation this week, recall the phrase "One little word shall fell him." Speak forth that word.
4. Examine your priorities in light of verse four. How do you feel about letting go of "goods . . . kindred . . . mortal life"?

The Prayer of the Heart

How hard, O Lord, for me to know you as "a bulwark never failing." My most trusted friends fail me. Human leaders are disgraced. Institutions crumble. Indeed, the whole cosmos seems in flux. Nothing is sure or secure. Nothing except you, O Lord. Perhaps this lack of fortresses in the created order will teach me all the more to walk by faith and not by sight, to trust you as my fortress. Amen.

Standing on the Promises

PROMISES (11.11.11.9. with refrain)

R. Kelso Carter, 1886

R. Kelso Carter, 1886

1. Stand-ing on the prom-is-es of Christ my King, Thro' e-ter-nal a-ges let His
2. Stand-ing on the prom-is-es that can-not fail, When the howl-ing storms of doubt and
3. Stand-ing on the prom-is-es of Christ the Lord, Bound to Him e-ter-nal-ly by
4. Stand-ing on the prom-is-es I can-not fall, Lis-t'ning ev-ery mo-ment to the

prais-es ring; Glo-ry in the high-est, I will shout and sing, Stand-ing on the prom-is-es of
fear as-sail, By the liv-ing Word of God I shall pre-vail, Stand-ing on the prom-is-es of
love's strong cord, O-ver-com-ing dai-ly with the Spir-it's sword, Stand-ing on the prom-is-es of
Spir-it's call, Rest-ing in my Sav-ior as my all in all, Stand-ing on the prom-is-es of

Refrain

God. Stand-ing, stand - ing, stand-ing on the prom-is-es of God my Sav-ior;
stand-ing on the prom-is-es,

Stand-ing, stand - ing, I'm stand-ing on the prom-is-es of God.
stand-ing on the prom-is-es,

Scripture Reading: 2 Peter 1:3–15

The second letter from Peter is, in effect, his "last will and testament" to the Church (v. 14). It contains, therefore, things of central importance to an ongoing life of discipleship to Jesus Christ. Notice his deep concern that we be free from the corruption that is in the world. Look at the infrastructure he gives for overcoming all manner of evil: faith and goodness and knowledge and self-control and endurance and godliness and mutual affection and love. Note, too, the way these build upon one another, with love being the culmination of the process.

Scripture Meditation: 2 Peter 1:4

[God] has given us . . . his precious and very great promises, so that through them you may escape from the corruption that is in the world because of lust, and may become participants of the divine nature.

As you meditate on this passage, look at the connection Peter makes between "precious promises" and freedom from corruption. Indeed, he states it in the most dramatic of terms, declaring that we become "participants of the divine nature."

Reflecting in Song

This spirited gospel song celebrates the "precious and very great promises" of God. Sing through the song, looking for the many facets of God's promises it affirms. Notice power is available to overcome even "the storms of doubt and fear."

Focus now on the first verse. It is a paean of praise to Jesus Christ in all his regal splendor. Notice how the songwriter does not hesitate to speak of the promises of God and the promises of Christ in the same breath. This is a very high Christology indeed, and it elicits in us the responses of shouting and singing. Allow yourself to be drawn into a joyful adoration of Jesus as you sing this verse over several times.

The second verse gives special attention to the power of the promises of God to overcome the "howling storms of doubt and fear." You may want to consider the various doubts and fears that dog your heels. Hold them up into the light of God's faithfulness and mercy. Watch them weaken and fade when exposed to the Light. Allow this verse to stay with you throughout

the day as you seek to walk in the Light as Jesus—the living Word of God—is in the Light (1 John 1:7).

In the third verse center on the metaphor of "love's strong cord." It is reminiscent of Hosea's "cords of compassion, bands of love." Many today think of commitments of any kind in a negative light. But consider the safety and security found in this commitment. And the power: through the bondage of love we are "overcoming daily by the Spirit's sword."

Meditate on the words *listening* and *resting* found in verse four. The two activities are connected in significant ways. When we live breathlessly, we do not listen well. Exhaustion does not lend itself to attentiveness. Sing through this verse quietly. Allow yourself to relax into the strong, safe, and secure arms of Jesus Christ.

Now, sing the entire song again and enjoy especially the refrain. Stand in the assurance of all of these "precious and very great promises" of God.

Questions of Examen and Exercises of Devotion

1. In what ways am I sustained by the promises of God?
2. Do I ever fret needlessly?
3. List a dozen statements in Scripture in which God has bound himself to maintain covenant with you. Sing the refrain of this song with these promises in mind.
4. This next week speak to one other person about your experience of the faithfulness of God.

The Prayer of the Heart

I think today, Lord Jesus, of your promise to love me and stay with me. I accept this as the bedrock foundation of my life, and I will bank everything on it. Amen.

To God Be the Glory

TO GOD BE THE GLORY (11.11.11.11. with refrain)

Fanny J. Crosby, 1875

William H. Doane, 1875

1. To God be the glo-ry, great things he hath done! So loved he the world that he gave us his Son, who yield-ed his life an a-tone-ment for sin, and o-pened the life-gate that all may go in.

Refrain

Praise the Lord, praise the Lord, let the earth hear his voice! Praise the Lord, praise the Lord, let the peo-ple re-joice! O come to the Fa-ther through Je-sus the Son, and give him the glo-ry, great things he hath done!

2. O perfect redemption, the purchase of blood,
   To every believer the promise of God;
   The vilest offender who truly believes,
   That moment from Jesus a pardon receives.

3. Great things he hath taught us, great things he hath done,
   And great our rejoicing through Jesus the Son;
   But purer, and higher, and greater will be
   Our wonder, our transport, when Jesus we see.

Scripture Reading: Psalm 96:1–6

So often in the Psalms when we are given a command to praise God, we are also given the reason for doing so. Observe that pattern here. Notice that the command is not just to praise, but also to proclaim—every day and every place—the salvation, the glory, and the greatness of God.

Scripture Meditation: Psalm 96:2–3

Sing to the LORD, bless his name;
tell of his salvation from day to day.
Declare his glory among the nations,
his marvelous works among all the peoples.

In meditating on this verse, focus in on the words *sing, bless, tell, declare.* Memorize these four verbs and let them be a framework for remembering the whole passage. Now, speak the opening lines of the song: "To God be the glory, great things he hath done! So loved he the world that he gave us his Son." Note how these lines fulfill the commands to "declare his glory" and "his marvelous works" and to "tell of his salvation." Sing the entire song.

Reflecting in Song

This hymn of praise and proclamation was written by Fanny Crosby, one of America's most well known hymn writers. She and her contemporaries developed the nineteenth-century gospel hymn, and Fanny was the most prolific writer of gospel hymn texts. She worked with D. L. Moody and Ira Sankey in their evangelistic campaigns, and Sankey credited his and Moody's success "more than any other human factor, to Fanny Crosby's hymns."[19]

Though blinded in infancy due to a doctor's mistake, Fanny did not give in to bitterness or self-pity. Rather, she rejoiced that "when I get to heaven, the first face that shall ever gladden my sight will be that of my Savior."[20] As a result of her blindness, Fanny developed a tremendous memory. She knew large portions of Scripture and classical poetry, and her own nine-thousand-plus hymns and poems were "written" in her mind, which she found to be more efficient than writing in braille. She loved to play the piano—everything from classical to ragtime—and she enjoyed "pepping things up" by playing old hymns in a jazzed-up style. Though small and frail, Fanny possessed boundless energy, and she continued to work and write, travel, and speak until she was past ninety.[21]

Fanny Crosby's name is closely associated with the Evangelical Tradition, but we can look to her as exemplary in any of the five Christian traditions because of the balanced life she led. This frail, blind woman lived voluntarily in the tenements of New York and did a great deal of personal ministry in the notorious Bowery district. She was said to possess an "irresistible charm and an indisputable holiness"—a holiness that brought about conversions wherever she went.[22] In the hours after midnight Fanny found quiet for periods of "deep meditation," during which she often received inspiration for her hymns, which she always credited to the "Blessed Holy Spirit." Fanny's hymns were much in demand, and she could have asked high prices for them, but she would accept only minimal fees from her publishers. Her one desire and prayer was that her hymns be used to "save a million souls."

Fanny Crosby was an accomplished poet who purposely incarnated her poetry for the masses, writing so the "man on the street"—or even in the gutter—could understand. For this she was ridiculed by the critics. But her hymns have endured, and many are now considered traditional classics.

"Don't tell a man he is a sinner," Fanny always insisted. "You can't save a man by telling him of his sins. He knows them already. Tell him there is pardon and love waiting for him. . . . That is all people want—love."[23] Sing the hymn once again. Proclaim, as Fanny Crosby did in both word and deed, the glory, the greatness, and the love of God.

Questions of Examen and Exercises of Devotion

1. In what way am I participating in the proclamation of the gospel?
2. Of whom do I think when I sing in verse two of "the vilest offender"? (Recall that in 1 Tim. 1:15 Paul considered himself the "foremost of sinners," RSV.)
3. Pray each day this week that God will show you someone whom you can "tell of his salvation."
4. Enjoy a Fanny Crosby week. Sing, worship, and meditate, using a different hymn of hers each day. (Most hymnals contain several, and any evangelical hymnal will have a wide selection.)

The Prayer of the Heart

"To God be the glory." Lord, I don't think I know how to give you glory. Is it by feeling exuberant or by saying certain words or by holding my head in a certain way? God, this song helps me realize that your glory is seen primarily in your goodness, your love. Perhaps having a heart of gratitude for these things is one way I give you glory. If so, then enlarge my capacity for gratitude. Amen.

Majesty

Jack Hayford

Jack Hayford

Maj - es - ty,————— wor - ship His maj - es - ty.————— Un - to Je - sus be all glo - ry, hon - or, and praise.————— Maj - es - ty,————— king - dom au - thor - i - ty flow from His throne un - to His own; His an - them raise.————— So ex - alt, lift up on high the name of Je - sus.————— Mag - ni - fy, come glo - ri - fy Christ Je - sus, the King. Maj - es - ty,————— wor - ship His maj - es - ty;————— Je - sus who died, now glo - ri - fied, King of all kings.—————

Accompaniment for this song is found on page 150.

Scripture Reading: Ephesians 1:3–23

In this passage, Paul delineates the many spiritual blessings that are ours in Christ. He follows up with a personal prayer of thanksgiving and intercession, that his readers might know the present reality of these things in their lives. As you read, take note of these blessings.

Scripture Meditation: Ephesians 1:18–19

[I pray that] you may know what is the hope to which he has called you, what are the riches of his glorious inheritance among the saints, and what is the immeasurable greatness of his power for us who believe.

In meditating on this Scripture, center one at a time on: the *hope* to which God has called you; the *riches* of his inheritance; the greatness of his *power*. Pray that you may know this hope, these riches, this power, in a new and tangible way. Sing this song and worship the all-sufficient Source of these gifts.

Reflecting in Song

"Majesty" is one of the most widely sung songs in the Christian world today. It was written in 1977 by the Reverend Jack Hayford. As he and his wife Anna were touring the British Isles, Pastor Hayford was impressed by the magnificent castles and symbols of royalty that were present in abundance. It caused him to reflect upon the regal majesty of Christ and the royal inheritance we enjoy as children of the King. Jack tells how one day as he and Anna drove along, "The opening lyrics and melody of 'Majesty' simply came to my heart."[24] As he continued to drive, Anna jotted the words and melody line in a notebook. Later, upon returning home, he completed the song. As you sing this song, travel in your mind's eye past some of those ancient castles and other places of regal splendor.

This beautiful hymn of worship declares the glorious majesty of our Lord Jesus Christ, and it serves to remind us that we, too, are royalty. We are "heirs of God and joint heirs with Christ" (Rom. 8:17). Because of our sovereign Lord, we share in the hope to which he has called us. It is hope for this life as well as eternal life—life with the King himself, whose presence and companionship we enjoy now and forever, and whose very glory we will someday share (Rom. 5:2). As royalty, we also partake in the riches of Christ's inheritance—an inheritance that includes "every spiritual blessing" and that, unlike earthly wealth, is undefiled and unfading (1 Peter 1:4). And as one of the King's own, we share in his power and authority. Jack Hayford reminds us that "our worship, when begotten in spirit and in truth, can align us with [Christ's] throne in such a way that His Kingdom authority flows to us—to overflow us, to free us and channel through us."[25]

Why does he give us this power and authority? Is it so we can exert influence, exercise control, or impress others? No. Jesus says, "All authority in heaven and on earth has been given to me. Go therefore and make disciples. . . ." (Matt. 28:18–19) It is so that we can lift up Christ, that he may be glorified and may draw all peoples to himself. It is so that his kingdom may come on earth, as it is in heaven. And it is so that our joy may be full (John 15:7–11), for whatever gives glory to the King brings joy to us. God's glory, our joy: the one gives rise to the other. This reality of the kingdom is just one of the many "spiritual blessings" of our heritage.

Sing the song once more. Take confidence in the fact that you are a child of the King. Rejoice in your hope and enjoy your inheritance. Claim your authority and proclaim his name. Worship his majesty!

Questions of Examen and Exercises of Devotion

1. How might my life change if I were the child of an earthly king?
2. How would my life change if I lived in a fuller realization of my royal heritage in Christ?
3. The refrain of an old gospel song says, "I'm a child of the King, a child of the King! With Jesus, my Savior, I'm a child of the King!"[26] Repeat (or sing) this phrase throughout the week as a reminder.
4. Is there one person you lovingly could speak to this week about the majesty of Jesus?

The Prayer of the Heart

Jesus, your love, your humanity, your sacrifice—all these elicit worship in me quickly. But majesty engenders more fear than worship. Your majesty speaks of distance and separation. And yet, O God, how true it is: you are the God who is wholly Other. The distance between creature and Creator is infinite. And the more I align myself with this truth, the more I will worship in Spirit and truth. Amen.

Crown Him with Many Crowns

Matthew Bridges, 1851 (vs. 1, 4–7); Godfrey Thring, 1874 (vs. 2–3)

DIADEMATA (S.M.D.)
George J. Elvey, 1868

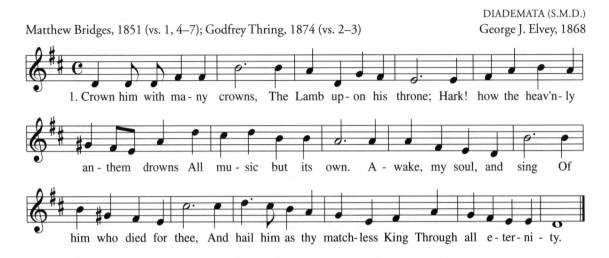

1. Crown him with ma-ny crowns, The Lamb up-on his throne; Hark! how the heav'n-ly an-them drowns All mu-sic but its own. A-wake, my soul, and sing Of him who died for thee, And hail him as thy match-less King Through all e-ter-ni-ty.

2. Crown him the Son of God
   Before the worlds began,
   And ye, who tread where he
     hath trod,
   Crown him the Son of man;
   Who every grief hath known
   That wrings the human breast,
   And takes and bears them for his
     own,
   That all in him may rest.

3. Crown him the Lord of life
   Who triumphed o'er the grave,
   And rose victorious in the
     strife
   For those he came to save.
   His glories now we sing
   Who died and rose on high,
   Who died, eternal life to bring,
   And lives that death may die.

4. Crown him the Lord of love,
   Behold his hands and side,
   Rich wounds yet visible above
   In beauty glorified.
   No angel in the sky
   Can fully bear that sight,
   But downward bends his
     burning eye
   At mysteries so bright.

5. Crown him the Lord of peace,
   Whose power a scepter sways
   From pole to pole that wars may
     cease,
   Absorbed in prayer and praise.
   His reign shall know no end,
   And round his piercèd feet
   Fair flowers of paradise
     extend
   Their fragrance ever sweet.

6. Crown him the Lord of years,
   The Potentate of time,
   Creator of the rolling spheres,
   Ineffably sublime.
   All hail, Redeemer, hail!
   For thou hast died for me;
   Thy praise and glory shall not
     fail
   Throughout eternity.

7. Crown him the Lord of heav'n,
   Enthroned in worlds above;
   Crown him the King, to whom
     is giv'n
   The wondrous name of Love.
   Crown him with many crowns,
   As thrones before him fall,
   Crown him, ye kings, with
     many crowns,
   For he is King of all.

Scripture Reading: Revelation 19:6–16
A grand and glorious celebration is taking place in heaven. The marriage feast of the Lamb has come at last! As you read, imagine yourself in the midst of this magnificent scene of rejoicing. Feel the reverberation of the heavenly anthem, which "drowns all music but its own." Notice throughout the passage the names given to Christ.

Scripture Meditation: Revelation 19:12a, 16

His eyes are like a flame of fire, and on his head are many diadems; . . . On his robe and on his thigh he has a name inscribed, "King of kings and Lord of lords."

As you focus on these verses, contemplate that supreme, majestic name, "King of kings and Lord of lords." Affirm Christ's Kingship and Lordship of heaven and earth, of your nation, your city, your neighborhood, your family, your life. Ask that it may be made manifest.

Reflecting in Song

This wonderful hymn of worship honors the many names, many crowns, many realms of Christ's Lordship. Based upon Revelation 19:12, it was originally written in 1851 by Matthew Bridges, an English hymn writer. Another Englishman, Godfrey Thring, later wrote additional verses, and since 1880 "Crown Him with Many Crowns" has been sung in various combinations of stanzas from both writers.[27] The tune was written by English organist and composer George Elvey expressly for this text and named "*Diademata*"— the Greek word for "crowns."

Read through these seven stanzas. Notice how each one focuses on a different realm of Christ's Lordship. Now, sing the first verse. Let it be a call to worship for the rest of the hymn: "Awake, my soul, and sing!"

Consider the second verse, which focuses on the incarnation. The Son of God not only came among us; he became one of us. He has "borne our griefs and carried our sorrows" (Isa. 53:4, RSV), and he sympathizes with our weakness, for he has been tested in every way as we have (Heb. 4:15). Sing this verse and worship the One "who every grief hath known / That wrings the human breast."

Turn your attention to verse three and the imagery of the Lord of life. Because of Christ, death itself is doomed, having been "swallowed up in victory" (1 Cor. 15:54). We not only have the assurance of eternal life; we have the reality of abundant life here and now. Sing this verse and "crown him the Lord of life."

Contemplate verse four, meditating on the Lord of love, whose hands and side still bear the marks of his rich, sacrificial love. The angels themselves cannot yet comprehend this love of God for sinful humanity, this mystery of redemption (1 Pet. 1:12). Sing the verse, and worship.

Now focus on verse five—the Lord of peace. "Peace? Where?" we might ask. Yes, earthly peace is promised. Though we cannot yet see it, there will come a day when "nation shall not lift up sword against nation, neither shall they learn war any more" (Isa. 2:4). But even now the Prince of Peace says, "Peace I leave with you; my peace I give to you. I do not give to you as the world gives" (John 14:27). Jesus gives peace within— peace with family and friends, even peace with enemies—when we let his kingdom rule in our lives. Sing, and crown him the Lord of peace.

Give attention to verse six. Reflect on this "Lord of years" to whom time itself is subject and for whom "one day is like a thousand years, and a thousand years are like one day" (2 Pet. 3:8). Sing, and worship him who is the same yesterday, today, and forever (Heb. 13:8).

Finally, look at verse seven. Christ is the Lord of all kingdoms, both in heaven and on earth. In him all were created, "whether thrones or dominions or rulers or powers" (Col. 1:16). From him all rulers receive their power, and to him every knee shall bow whether in heaven or on earth or under the earth (Phil. 2:10). Sing this verse. Worship him, proclaim him, crown him with many crowns, for he is King of all!

Questions of Examen and Exercises of Devotion

1. Which area of Christ's Lordship mentioned in the hymn is most real to me? Which is most difficult to acknowledge?

2. Besides those mentioned in this hymn, what are some other realms of his Lordship?

3. Each of these seven stanzas is replete with material for meditation. Focus on a different one each day for a week and reflect on that particular aspect of Christ's Lordship.

4. Begin each of the next several days with the phrase, "Awake, my soul, and sing of him who died for thee."

The Prayer of the Heart

O regal, glorious King Jesus, I do not have many crowns. Only one, the crown of my life. Compared to the realms of splendor over which you rule, it is a puny crown indeed. But I gladly offer it to you. Enabled by your Spirit, I crown you the Lord of my life. Thank you for receiving this simple offering. Amen.

About RENOVARÉ

Our Mission: RENOVARÉ is committed to working for the renewal of the Church of Jesus Christ in all its multifaceted expressions.

Our Character: RENOVARÉ is Christian in commitment, international in scope, and ecumenical in breadth. We seek to fulfill our mission by combining a balanced vision that incorporates the best from the five Christian traditions with a practical strategy that utilizes such things as small group meetings, national and local conferences, one-day seminars, personal and group retreats, reading devotional classics for spiritual growth and enrichment, and long-term commitment to renewal.

The following are the five great traditions, or streams, of Christian life and faith to which we refer:

Contemplative: The Prayer-Filled Life focuses upon intimacy with God and depth of spirituality. This spiritual dimension addresses the longing for a deeper, more vital Christian experience.

Holiness: The Virtuous Life focuses upon personal moral transformation and the power to develop "holy habits." This spiritual dimension addresses the erosion of moral fiber in the contemporary Church.

Charismatic: The Spirit-Empowered Life focuses upon the charisms of the Spirit and worship. This spiritual dimension addresses the yearning for the immediacy of God's presence among his people.

Social Justice: The Compassionate Life focuses upon justice and shalom in all human relationships and social structures. This spiritual dimension addresses the gospel imperative for equity and compassion among all peoples.

Evangelical: The Word-Centered Life focuses upon the centrality of Christ and the importance of Scripture. This spiritual dimension addresses the need for a center of certainty in the Christian life and faith.

Our Covenant: We invite everyone everywhere to join us by committing themselves to the following covenant:

In utter dependence upon Jesus Christ as my everliving Savior, Teacher, Lord, and Friend, I will seek continual renewal through:

- spiritual exercises,
- spiritual gifts, and
- acts of service.

Our Common Disciplines: The following common disciplines, based upon the five great streams of life in Christian faith and witness, give substance to our daily living of the RENOVARÉ Covenant. In addition to these, we encourage individuals and groups to develop other specific spiritual disciplines that are appropriate to their particular situation.

The Prayer-Filled Life: I will set aside time regularly for prayer, meditation, and spiritual reading and will seek to practice the presence of God.

The Virtuous Life: By God's grace, I will strive mightily against sin, and will do deeds of love and mercy that lead to righteousness.

The Spirit-Empowered Life: I will seek the gifts of the Holy Spirit, nurturing the fruit and experiencing the joy and power of the Spirit.

The Compassionate Life: I will seek to serve others everywhere I can and will work for justice in all human relationships and social structures.

The Word-Centered Life: I will study the Scriptures regularly and share my faith with others as God leads.

Spiritual Formation Groups: These groups are at the heart of the RENOVARÉ experience. Gathering for the purpose of mutual nurture and encouragement, they center on the Covenant, the Common Disciplines, and related Self-Examination Questions. All people in the group are committed to the spiritual growth of one another. For more information about Spiritual Formation Groups, see *A Spiritual Formation Workbook* by James Bryan Smith (San Francisco: HarperSanFrancisco, 1993). For more information about RENOVARÉ, write to RENOVARÉ, 8 Inverness Drive East, Suite 102, Englewood, CO 80112-5609.

Accompaniments for Selected Songs

Come Home

(The Father's Invitation)

Miriam Overholt   Miriam Overholt

Lyrics:

1. My heart is o-pen wide._____ I long_____ to find you near._____
My arms are stretched to re-ceive_____ you whom I hold dear._____

2. No long-er stand out-side._____ Come through the door of grace,_____
To know and be ful-ly known, To dwell in my em - brace._____

Jesus, Take Me as I Am

D. Bryant

D. Bryant

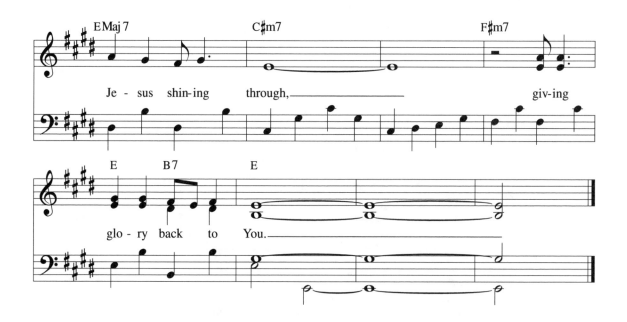

Je - sus shin-ing   through,_____   giv-ing

glo - ry back   to   You._____

Kyrie Eleison
Setting 3

Ancient Greek Text

From "Mass in G" by Franz Schubert (1797–1828)

Adapt. by Janet L. Janzen

Gently flowing

Ky - ri - e   e - le - i - son.

Ky - ri - e   e - le - i - son.

Fill Me with Your Spirit

Janet L. Janzen

Janet L. Janzen

1. Fill me with your Spir - it and take Him not a - way.

Fill me with your pow - er to walk in your way. (fill me)

Fill me with your love; let me love you more to - day.

Fill me, Lord Je - sus, I pray.

Spirit Song

John Wimber, 1979

SPIRIT SONG (9.7.11.D. with refrain)
John Wimber, 1979

1. O let the Son of God en-fold you with his Spir-it and his
(2. O come and) sing this song with glad-ness as your hearts are filled with

love. Let him fill your heart and sat-is-fy your soul.
joy. Lift your hands in sweet sur-ren-der to his name.

O let him have the things that hold you, and his Spir-it like a
O give him all your tears and sad-ness; give him all your years of

dove will de-scend up-on your life and make you whole.
pain, and you'll en-ter in-to life in Je-sus' name.

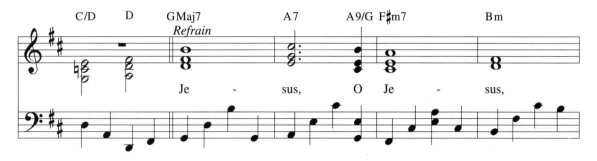

C/D   D   GMaj7   A7   A9/G   F♯m7   Bm

Refrain

Je - sus,   O   Je - sus,

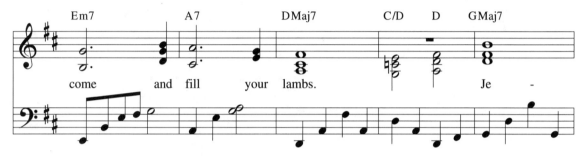

Em7   A7   DMaj7   C/D   D   GMaj7

come   and   fill   your   lambs.   Je -

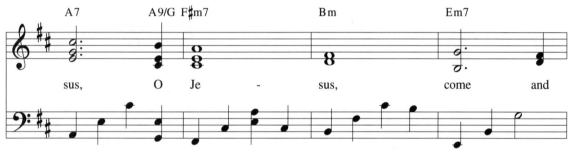

A7   A9/G   F♯m7   Bm   Em7

sus,   O   Je - sus,   come   and

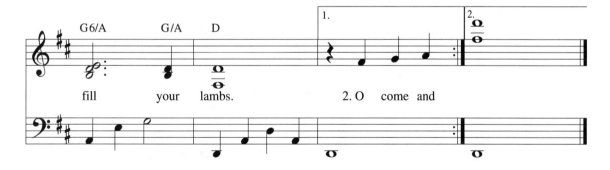

G6/A   G/A   D   1.   2.

fill   your   lambs.   2. O   come and

We Pray for Peace

Ken Medema

Ken Medema

love comes down like a sum - mer rain; 'til the riv - ers of jus - tice

flow a - gain, 'til the day of ju - bi - lee is come, We

pray for peace up - on our plan - et home.

Let Justice Roll

Prayer of St. Francis

Attr. to St. Francis of Assisi (1182–1226); Paraphrased by Janet L. Janzen

Janet L. Janzen

Our Father

Miriam Overholt

Miriam Overholt

Freely, as a chant

1. Je - sus the on - ly Son of God, In - car - nate Word sent from the
2. God, you who formed us by your Word, cre - a - ting life it - self with -
3. Spir - it, the ve - ry life of God, the liv - ing Word em - bod - ied

Fa - ther, You in your - self be - came the way for us to
in us, Source of hope and giv - er of good gifts, we long to
in us, Breathe on our hearts un - til we feel our pulse be -

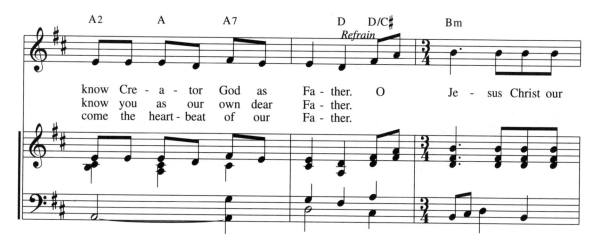

I Will Change Your Name

D. J. Butler

A Mighty Fortress

Setting 2

EIN' FESTE BURG (8.7.8.7.5.5.5.6.7.)

Martin Luther, ca. 1529; Tr. composite

Martin Luther, ca. 1529

1. A might-y for-tress is our God, a bul-wark nev-er fail - ing;
Our help-er he, a-mid the flood of mor-tal ills pre-vail - ing.
The old___ e - vil foe now means dead-ly woe; Deep guile and great might
are his dread arms in fight; On earth is not his e - qual.

2. Did we in our own strength confide our striving would be losing;
Were not the right Man on our side, the Man of God's own choosing.
Ask ye, Who is this? Jesus Christ it is,
Of Sabaoth Lord, and there's none other God;
He holds the field forever.

Shine, Jesus, Shine

Graham Kendrick

Graham Kendrick

1. Lord, the light of your love is shin- ing in the midst of the
2. Lord, I come to your awe- some pres- ence, from the shad- ows in-
3. As we gaze on your king- ly bright- ness, so our fac- es dis-

dark- ness, shin- ing; Je- sus, Light of the World, shine up- on us,
to your ra- diance; by the blood I may en- ter your bright- ness,
play your like- ness, ev- er chang- ing from glo- ry to glo- ry,

set us free by the truth you now bring us: Shine on me,
search me, try me, con- sume all my dark- ness: Shine on me,
mir- rored here may our lives tell your sto- ry: Shine on me,

Majesty

Jack Hayford

Jack Hayford

Maj - es - ty,_____ wor-ship His maj - es - ty._____ Un - to
Je - sus be all glo - ry, hon - or, and praise._____
Maj - es - ty,_____ king-dom au - thor - i - ty_____ flow from His
throne un - to His own; His an - them raise._____ So ex -

Credits

Listed below are the names and addresses of the copyright owners whose property appears in this book. Their permission grants are restricted to this book and all copyrighted property is included here with the permission of these owners. No further use of this copyrighted property may be made without obtaining the permission of the owner. Every effort has been made to locate the owners of the copyrighted material that appears here. Any omissions are regretted and all necessary corrections will be made in subsequent printings.

"Gloria Patri (Glory Be to the Father)" Copyright © 1994; "Be Thou My Vision" verse 3 Copyright © 1991; *"Kyrie Eleison* (Lord, Have Mercy" setting one music Copyright © 1993 and setting three arrangement Copyright © 1994; "Fill Me With Your Spirit" Copyright © 1990; "Prayer of St. Francis" Copyright © 1993; "Whatever You Do" Copyright © 1994; all by Janet Lindeblad Janzen, c/o RENOVARÉ, 8 Inverness Drive East, Suite 102, Englewood, CO 80112–5609.

"As the Deer" by Martin Nystrom. Copyright © 1984 MARANATHA! MUSIC. (Adm. by The Copyright Co., Nashville, TN.) All rights reserved. International copyright secured. Used by permission.

"More Precious than Silver" by Lynn DeShazo. Copyright © 1982 Integrity's Hosanna! Music, c/o Integrity Music, Inc., P. O. Box 851622, Mobile, AL 36685. All rights reserved. International copyright secured. Used by permission.

"Stay with Me" by Jacques Berthier. Copyright © 1982, 1983, and 1984, Les Presses de Taizé (France). Used by permission of G.I.A. Publications, Inc., Chicago, IL, exclusive agent. All rights reserved.

"Precious Lord, Take My Hand" words and music by Thomas A. Dorsey. Copyright © 1938 by Unichappell Music, Inc. Adm. by Hal Leonard Corporation. Copyright renewed. International copyright secured. All rights reserved.

"Come Home (The Father's Invitation)" and "Our Father," Copyright © Miriam Kline Overholt, c/o Church of the Savior, 875 Spaulding, Wichita, KS 67203.

"Jesus, Take Me as I Am" by David Bryant. Copyright © 1978 Thankyou Music/Adm. in N., C., and S. America by Integrity's Hosanna! Music, c/o Integrity Music, Inc., P. O. Box 851622, Mobile, AL 36685. All rights reserved. International copyright secured. Used by permission.

"Holy Ground" by Christopher Beatty, Copyright © 1982 and this arr. © 1986 Birdwing Music/Cherry Lane Music Publishing Co., Inc. Admin. by EMI Christian Music Publishing. All rights reserved. Reprinted by permission.

"Hide Me in Your Holiness" by Steve Ragsdale. Copyright © 1986. MARANATHA! MUSIC. (Adm. by The Copyright Co., Nashville, TN.) All rights reserved. International copyright secured. Used by permission.

"Change My Heart, Oh God" by Eddie Espinosa. Copyright © 1982 Mercy Publishing (adm. by Music Services). International copyright secured. All rights reserved. Used by permission.

"How Majestic Is Your Name" by Michael W. Smith. Copyright © Meadowgreen Music Company, admin. by EMI Christian Music Publishing. All rights reserved. Reprinted by permission.

"In the Presence of Your People (The Celebration Song)" by Brent Chambers. Copyright © 1977. Scripture In Song (adm. by MARANATHA! MUSIC c/o The Copyright Co., Nashville, TN). All rights reserved. International copyright secured. Used by permission.

"Spirit Song" by John Wimber. Copyright © 1979, Mercy Publishing (adm. by Music Services). International copyright secured. All rights reserved. Used by permission.

"The Trees of the Field" by Steffi Geiser Rubin & Stuart Dauermann. Copyright © 1975 Lillenas Publishing Company/SESAC. All rights reserved. Adm. by Integrated Copyright Group, Inc.

"We Pray for Peace" and "Let Justice Roll" by Ken Medema. Copyright © 1993 Ken Medema Music/ASCAP/Brier Patch Music. All rights reserved. Used by permission.

"Ubi Caritas (Where There Is Charity)" by Jacques Berthier. Copyright © 1978, 1980, and 1981 Les Presses de Taizé (France). Used by permission of G.I.A. Publications, Inc., Chicago, IL, exclusive agent. All rights reserved.

"Here I Am, Lord" by Daniel L. Schutte. Copyright © 1981, Daniel L. Schutte and New Dawn Music, P. O. Box 13248, Portland, OR 97213. All rights reserved. Used with permission.

"I Will Change Your Name" by D. J. Butler. Copyright © 1987, Mercy Publishing (adm. by Music Services). International copyright secured. All rights reserved. Used by permission.

"Shine, Jesus, Shine" by Graham Kendrick. Copyright © 1987 Make Way Music/Adm. in N., C., and S. America by Integrity's Hosanna! Music, c/o Integrity Music, Inc., P. O. Box 851622, Mobile, AL 36685. All rights reserved. International copyright secured. Used by permission.

"Majesty" by Jack W. Hayford. Copyright © 1981, Rocksmith Music, c/o Trust Music Management, Inc., P. O. Box 9256, Calabasas, CA 91372. Used by permission. All rights reserved.

Notes

The Call of the Heart

1. The chorale melodies came from a variety of sources: sacred and secular folk songs, plainsong of the Roman church, and contemporary Protestant composers. Bach himself wrote very few original chorale melodies, but the chorales of the Reformation provided the raw material for his compositions, as they have for composers ever since.

2. In order to differentiate between the two styles commonly referred to as "gospel," we use the term *gospel hymn* or *gospel song* in reference to the style of music that grew out of the nineteenth-century revivals under the leadership of Ira Sankey and P. P. Bliss, and *Gospel music* (capital *G*) in reference to the black gospel style that developed in the 1920s under the leadership of Thomas Dorsey. See "Precious Lord, Take My Hand," also the Selected Resources section for more on the development of both kinds of gospel music.

3. Quoted by David Appleby, *History of Church Music* (Chicago: Moody, 1965), 23.

4. *The Confessions of St. Augustine,* trans. John K. Ryan (Garden City, NY: Doubleday, 1960), 261.

Introduction

1. As quoted by James R. Sydnor in "The Hymn Society's New Hymnal," *The Hymn: A Journal of Congregational Song* 44, no. 3 (July 1993): 8–9.

2. Exactly what kind of sacred text, poem, or song constitutes a true hymn (that is, what elements must be included, what type of music is suitable, and so forth) has been debated throughout the centuries from Augustine to the present. In the Scriptures, Paul refers to "psalms, hymns, and spiritual songs" (Eph. 5:19 and Col. 3:16). Some have sought to categorize sacred song accordingly, and the Church has been divided over the singing of "hymns" as opposed to

"psalms" (see "Joy to the World"). We understand Paul's words to mean, not a strict system of classification, but rather that there is to be variety in our styles and expressions of Christian song.

3. The meter is simply the number of syllables in each line of a text fitting that tune; for example, AURELIA, 7.6.7.6.D. is the tune commonly used for "The Church's One Foundation." (The *D* stands for "double," meaning eight lines instead of four.) Certain frequently used meters are designated by letters such as C.M. or L.M., with C.M. being Common Meter, which is 8.6.8.6., and L.M. being Long Meter, which is 8.8.8.8. Most hymnals have a metrical index identifying these and listing all of the hymns according to meter. The metrical index is useful if you want to find a different tune to fit a given text, and vice versa.

4. We are offering a tape in conjunction with this book (see Selected Resources). It is intended, not as an accompaniment or as a substitute for singing the songs yourself, but rather as a teaching tool for those who learn music more readily by ear than by sight.

5. Some would regard this counsel as hymnological heresy. And it is true that a good hymn expresses a complete thought or a progression of thought. But it is also true that many of our hymns, especially older ones, do not appear in their entirety anyway, having already been cut, altered, or rearranged (see "O for a Thousand Tongues to Sing"). And as the product of editors' and committees' opinions, the stanzas may vary from one book to another.

6. From "O Holy Spirit, Enter In."

Songs of Confession

The Apostles' Creed

1. Quoted by Roland Bainton, *Here I Stand* (New York: Abingdon-Cokesbury, 1950), 337.

Jesus Loves Me

2. Anna B. Warner, *Say and Seal*, written in collaboration with her sister Susan.

3. The verses used here are as they appear in *Gospel Hymns (Consolidated)* (New York and Chicago: Biglow & Main, 1886; Cincinnati and New York: John Church, 1886).

Amazing Grace

4. John Newton, *Letters of a Slave Trader Freed by God's Grace,* paraphrased by Dick Bohrer (Chicago: Moody, 1983), 48.

5. Newton, *Letters of a Slave Trader,* 119.

In the Name of Christ We Gather

6. Quoted in *Source Readings in Music History,* selected and annotated by Oliver Strunk (New York: W. W. Norton, 1950), 65.

Songs of Contemplation

More Precious than Silver

1. Basilea Schlink, *My All for Him* (Minneapolis: Dimension, 1971), 25.

O Sacred Head, Now Wounded

2. Martin Luther, "Meditation on Christ's Passion," excerpt from *Devotional Writings,* ed. Martin O. Dietrich (Philadelphia: Fortress, 1969), 1:8–13.

In the Garden

3. Emily Herman, excerpts from *The Secret Garden of the Soul and Other Devotional Studies,* reprinted in *The Fellowship of the Saints,* ed. Thomas S. Kepler (New York: Abingdon-Cokesbury, 1948), 593–94.

Jesus, I Am Resting, Resting

4. *The Confessions of St. Augustine,* trans. John K. Ryan (Garden City, NY: Doubleday, 1960), 43.

5. John Calvin, *Commentaries on the Epistle of Paul the Apostle to the Romans,* trans. and ed. John Owen (Grand Rapids, MI: Eerdmans, 1947), 451.

Precious Lord, Take My Hand

6. Harry Eskew, *Handbook to the Baptist Hymnal* (Nashville: Convention Press, 1992), 329.

7. As quoted in *Handbook to the Baptist Hymnal,* 222.

Come Home (The Father's Invitation)

8. Richard J. Foster, *Prayer: Finding the Heart's True Home* (San Francisco: HarperSanFrancisco, 1992), 1.

9. Foster, *Prayer,* 1.

Songs of Holiness

Come, Ye Sinners, Poor and Needy

1. William Wilberforce, *Real Christianity,* abridged and ed. from 1829 edition by James M. Houston (Portland, OR: Multnomah, 1982), 13.

2. As quoted by R. G. McCutchan in *Our Hymnody* (New York: Abingdon-Cokesbury, 1937), 234.

Kyrie Eleison (Lord, Have Mercy)

3. The *Kyrie* has been sung in many different musical forms, including the plainsong of antiquity, the German *leise*—sacred folk songs of the Middle Ages so named because they used *kyrieleison* as a refrain—and the great choral works by composers such as Bach, Mozart, and Beethoven as a part of the Mass.

4. Pronounced "Key'-ree-eh eh-leh'-ee-sohn, Krees'-teh eh-leh'-ee-sohn."

5. Basilea Schlink, *Repentance: The Joy-filled Life* (Grand Rapids, MI: Zondervan, 1968), 15.

6. Schlink, *Repentance,* 14.

Nothing but the Blood of Jesus

7. See "Joy to the World" for further comment on antiphonal singing.

8. Elisabeth Elliot, "Making Your Marriage Work" series, "Gateway to Joy" radio program produced by Good News Broadcasting Assn., Inc., Lincoln, NE, Feb. 15, 1994.

I Lay My Sins on Jesus

9. "Cast Thy Burden upon the Lord," from Mendelssohn's oratorio *Elijah* (1847). Mendelssohn also used the tune in one of his *Songs Without Words* (bk. 3, no. 6). Bach used this tune with variations in Cantatas 24 and 71.

10. See "Joy to the World" for notes on psalm singing. Hymn singing came officially to Scotland even later than it did to England. The first hymnal of the Church of Scotland did not appear until 1898.

Bonar was in the Free Church of Scotland, which had a more accepting attitude, but "hymns of human composure" still were not considered proper for public worship. Thus, many of Bonar's hymns were written as devotional verse, and his children's songs were sung in more informal situations. When near the end of his life Bonar used one of his hymns in his own church, two elders walked out in protest!

Jesus, Take Me as I Am

11. *George MacDonald: Selections from His Greatest Works,* comp. David L. Neuhouser (Wheaton, IL: Victor Books/Scripture Press, 1990), 170.

Holy Ground

12. William Law, "A Serious Call to a Devout and Holy Life," *Devotional Classics,* ed. Richard J. Foster and James B. Smith (San Francisco: HarperSanFrancisco, 1993), 191.

13. Martin Luther, *The Martin Luther Christmas Book,* trans. and arr. Roland H. Bainton (Philadelphia: Fortress, 1968), 43.

Hide Me in Your Holiness

14. Martin Luther, *"simul justus et peccator"*: at the same time righteous and sinful.

15. *George MacDonald,* comp. Neuhouser, 42.

Change My Heart, O God

16. Thomas More, "A Devout Prayer," from *The Fellowship of the Saints,* comp. Thomas S. Kepler (New York and Nashville: Abingdon-Cokesbury, 1948), 256.

May the Mind of Christ My Savior

17. A. W. Tozer, *The Pursuit of God* (Camp Hill, PA: Christian Publications, 1982), 67.

18. C. S. Lewis, *The Screwtape Letters* (New York: Macmillan, 1961), 63.

19. George MacDonald, *A Daughter's Devotion,* rev. ed. of *Mary Marston* (1881), ed. Michael R. Phillips (Minneapolis: Bethany, 1988), 44.

Trust and Obey

20. Story from Ira Sankey, *My Life and the Story of the Gospel Hymns* (Philadelphia: Sunday School Times, 1907), 326.

21. *George MacDonald,* comp. Neuhouser, 102.

22. *George MacDonald,* comp. Neuhouser, 107.

Songs of the Spirit

How Majestic Is Your Name

1. O. Hallesby, *Prayer,* trans. Clarence J. Carlsen (Minneapolis: Augsburg, 1931), 141.

2. *The Book of Confessions: Presbyterian Church (USA)* (New York: Office of the General Assembly, 1983), no. 7.001.

3. As quoted by William A. Seaman in *Companion to the Hymnal of the Service Book and Hymnal* (Minneapolis: American Lutheran Church, and Philadelphia: Lutheran Church in America, 1976), 2.

Jubilate Deo (Rejoice in God)

4. Pronounced "yoo-bee-lah'-teh deh'-oh."

5. "Rejoice, Ye Pure in Heart," text by Edward H. Plumptre, 1865, and music by Arthur H. Messiter, 1883. It is found in many current hymnals.

6. Martin Luther, "Commentary on Psalm 147" (1531) from *Luther's Works,* ed. Jaroslav Pelikan (St. Louis, MO: Concordia, 1958), 14:111.

In the Presence of Your People (The Celebration Song)

7. St. John Chrysostom, from the "Exposition of Psalm XLI," *Source Readings in Music History,* selected and annotated by Oliver Strunk (New York: W. W. Norton, 1950), 68.

8. John Wesley, "Directions for Singing," from *Select Hymns,* 1761, reprinted in *The United Methodist Hymnal* (Nashville: United Methodist Publishing House, 1989), vii.

9. *The Confessions of St. Augustine,* trans. John K. Ryan (Garden City, NY: Doubleday, 1960), 214.

Fill Me with Your Spirit

10. Francis A. Schaeffer, *The Church Before the Watching World* (Downers Grove, IL: InterVarsity, 1971), 63.

11. Schaeffer, *Church Before the Watching World,* 63 (italics added).

12. Francis A. Schaeffer, "The Lord's Work in the Lord's Way," from *No Little People* (Downers Grove, IL: InterVarsity, 1974), 64.

Spirit Song

13. Elisabeth Elliot, "Gateway to Joy" radio program, various radio talks produced by Good News Broadcasting Assn., Inc., Lincoln, NE.

14. George MacDonald, *The Gamer's Awakening,* ed. Michael R. Phillips (Minneapolis: Bethany, 1983), 200.

15. Julian of Norwich, *Showings,* in *The Classics of Western Spirituality,* trans. Edmund Colledge and James Walsh (New York: Paulist, 1978). *Showings* is sometimes titled *Revelations of Divine Love.* Selections from it are included in *Devotional Classics.*

Joy to the World

16. Thomas Mace, as quoted by L. David Miller in *Hymns: The Story of Christian Song* (Philadelphia: Lutheran Church Press, 1969), 85.

17. Although "hymns of human composure" began to be more widely accepted after Watts's time, for many years they were sung only by those on the fringes of organized religion, that is, Dissenters and Methodists. The Church of England did not officially approve the singing of hymns in worship until 1820. See *Christian History* issue 31, vol. 10, no. 3, 35.

The Trees of the Field

18. Isidore of Seville, from the *Etymologiarum,* reprinted in *Source Readings in Music History,* selected and annotated by Oliver Strunk (New York: W. W. Norton, 1950), 94. See also "This Is My Father's World."

19. Alice Parker, *Melodious Accord: Good Singing in Church* (Chicago: Liturgy Training Publications, 1991), 12.

20. Elisabeth Elliot, *On Asking God Why* (Old Tappan, NJ: Power Books/Fleming H. Revell, 1989), 133.

Songs of Shalom

Down by the Riverside

1. Another characteristic of the African American spiritual was its double meaning. One meaning applied to everyday life and was a form of communication. Since slaves were not allowed to talk as they worked in the field, they used code words in their songs in order to communicate with each other. The other meaning of the song conveyed spiritual truths by which slaves offered empathy, encouragement, and hope to one another. Following and interpreting this use of "mask and symbol" in the spirituals is a study in itself. See "*Somebody's Calling My Name,*"

by Wyatt T. Walker (Valley Forge, PA: Judson, 1979), 56, 58.

Prayer of St. Francis

2. The actual origin of this prayer is unknown, but it is traditionally attributed to St. Francis of Assisi, and it certainly embodies his spirit.

Whatever You Do

3. George MacDonald, *A Daughter's Devotion,* rev. ed. of *Mary Marston* (1881), ed. Michael R. Phillips (Minneapolis: Bethany, 1988), 286.

Simple Gifts

4. A. W. Tozer, *The Pursuit of God* (Camp Hill, PA: Christian Publications, 1982), 22.

This Is My Father's World

5. As quoted by Ian Crofton, in *A Dictionary of Musical Quotations* (New York: Macmillan/ Schirmer Books, 1985), 140. See also "The Trees of the Field."

6. As quoted by Roland Bainton, *Here I Stand* (New York: Abingdon-Cokesbury, 1950), 221.

Ubi Caritas *(Where There Is Charity)*

7. See "Stay with Me."

8. Pronounced "Oo'-bee kah'-ree-tahs eht ah'-mor, deh'-oos eē'-bee ehst."

In Christ There Is No East or West

9. From an anonymous Letter to Diognetus, possibly dating from the second century, *A Lion Handbook: The History of Christianity,* ed. Dr. Tim Dowley (Batavia, IL: Lion Publishing, 1977), 67.

10. Prayer letter, Dr. Dean and Gretchen Samuelson (June 1994).

11. Dietrich Bonhoeffer, *Life Together,* trans. John W. Doberstein (San Francisco: Harper & Row, 1954), 23.

Here I Am, Lord

12. See *Monganga Paul: The Congo Ministry and Martyrdom of Paul Carlson, M.D.,* by Lois Carlson (New York: Harper & Row, 1966). Currently out of print but available in some libraries and used bookstores. Additional information in *Life* (Dec. 4, 1964), *Time* (Dec. 4, 1964), and *Newsweek* (Nov. 30, 1964).

13. Dean Samuelson, as quoted by Sharon Hamrick, in *The Wichita Eagle* (Nov. 9, 1991).

Songs of the Word

All Hail the Power of Jesus' Name

1. Charles Wesley, "Jesus! the Name," from *Hymns II* (Downers Grove, IL: InterVarsity, 1976), 45.

2. As quoted by E. E. Ryden, *The Story of Our Hymns,* (Rock Island, IL: Augustana, 1930), 240.

I Will Change Your Name

3. Song by Buck and Anne Herring and Matthew Ward, "That's Not Nice to Say," The Second Chapter of Acts from *Nightlight,* compact disc (Lindale, TX: Live Oak Records, 1985).

Shine, Jesus, Shine

4. "Hold My Heart," by Annie Herring from *Waiting for My Ride to Come,* compact disc (Brentwood, TN: Sparrow, 1991).

5. Malcolm Muggeridge, *Christ and the Media* (Grand Rapids, MI: Eerdmans, 1977), 77.

O for a Thousand Tongues to Sing

6. *The Journal of Rev. Charles Wesley,* extracts from the 1909 edition (Taylors, SC: The Methodist Reprint Society, 1977), 149.

7. We offer here fifteen of the original eighteen stanzas. In 1767 this hymn appeared in a hymnbook by R. Conyers with five of these stanzas, beginning with our stanza six (originally stanza seven). John Wesley, in his hymnal of 1780, continued to use that stanza as the first. He changed "my dear Redeemer" to "my great Redeemer" and placed the original first stanza ("Glory to God . . .") last. The number and arrangement of stanzas used continues to vary, but this sixth stanza ("O for a Thousand Tongues . . .") is normally placed first.

8. Charles Wesley wrote nearly nine thousand poems. Of these, over sixty-five hundred are generally considered to be hymns.

9. Henry Moore, as quoted by Timothy Dudley-Smith, *Christian History* issue 31, vol. 10, no. 3: 13.

10. Charles Wesley, as quoted by Dudley-Smith, *Christian History* issue 31, vol. 10, no. 3: 10.

11. Charles remained faithful to the Church of England though many Methodists advocated separation from the established church.

A Mighty Fortress

12. Martin Luther, "Commentary on Psalm 68 (1521)," *Luther's Works,* ed. Ulrich S. Leupold (Philadelphia: Fortress, 1965), 13:37.

13. Luther, "Concerning an Order of Public Worship (1523)," *Luther's Works,* ed. Leupold, 53:14.

14. Luther, "Preface to Georg Rhau's *Symphoniae iucundae* (1538)," *Luther's Works,* ed. Leupold, 53:323.

15. As quoted by R. G. McCutchan, *Our Hymnody* (New York: Abingdon-Cokesbury, 1937), 97.

16. The musical setting given on page 116 is the one most commonly used today. The melody as Luther wrote it was rhythmically more complex and followed the speech pattern of the text. It is found on page 147. There is speculation as to how hymns were actually sung in Luther's time (some believe his rhythms as written would have been too difficult for the average congregation), but indications are that the sixteenth-century German chorales were sung in the lively, polyrhythmic style in which they were notated. They would sound syncopated and almost jazzy to our ears. In the eighteenth century these melodies were evened out and written in their current isometric form with accompanying four-part harmony. See introduction to "The Hymns," *Luther's Works,* ed. Leupold, 53:204–205.

17. Ryden, *Story of Our Hymns,* 47.

18. As quoted by Richard Dinwiddie, "When You Sing Next Sunday, Thank Luther," *Christianity Today* (Oct. 21, 1983).

To God Be the Glory

19. Bernard Ruffin, *Fanny Crosby* (Westwood, NJ: Barbour & Co., 1976), 15.

20. As quoted by Ryden, *Story of Our Hymns,* 439.

21. Fanny Crosby died in 1915 at the age of 94.

22. Ruffin, *Fanny Crosby,* 187.

23. Ruffin, *Fanny Crosby,* 136.

Majesty

24. As quoted by David W. Music, *Handbook to the Baptist Hymnal* (Nashville: Convention Press, 1992), 187.

25. As quoted by Kenneth W. Osbeck, *Amazing Grace: 366 Inspiring Hymn Stories for Daily Devotions* (Grand Rapids, MI: Kregel, 1990), 273.

16. "A Child of the King" by Harriet E. Buell (1834–1910), ("My Father is rich in houses and lands . . .").

Crown Him with Many Crowns

27. *Thring's Church of England Hymn Book* (1880) was the first to combine the versions. Hymnal editors since then have continued to use stanzas from both authors in various combinations. Our seven verses are a compilation taken from the *Service Book and Hymnal,* Lutheran Church in America (Minneapolis, MN: Augsburg, 1958), no. 431, and *The Hymnal–1940,* Episcopal (New York: Church Pension Fund, 1940), no. 352.

Selected Resources

These resources were selected either because they were useful in compiling this book or because we feel they would be helpful in furthering your devotional use of hymns and songs. We hope that through them you might enjoy more of our diverse heritage of Christian song. A variety of Christian denominations and traditions are represented here. Their inclusion is not necessarily an endorsement of every point of doctrine contained therein. We would urge you to test *all* things, including these, by the Word of God, to take what is helpful and edifying to you, and to leave the rest.

Audiotape

Songs of Renewal audiotape. Made especially for use with this book, it includes some of the newly published or less-familiar songs. It is intended as a teaching tool for those who learn music more readily by ear than by sight. Available from RENOVARÉ, 8 Inverness Drive East, Suite 102, Englewood, CO 80112-5609 for a suggested donation of $10.00.

Hymnals

Note: These hymnals are not necessarily the latest editions. Many denominations have issued new hymnals in the past two decades. We feel that the older hymnals are valuable as well. The Hymn Society Book Service (see below) offers a comprehensive selection of the most recent hymnals.

The Baptist Hymnal. Southern Baptist Convention. Nashville: Convention Press, 1991. Contemporary hymns and gospel songs, praise choruses, and traditional hymns of the evangelical persuasion.

The Covenant Hymnal. Evangelical Covenant Church. Chicago: Covenant, 1973. Traditional and contemporary hymns, chorales, and gospel songs. Contains a wealth of Scandinavian hymnody.

The Hymnal for Worship and Celebration. Waco, TX: Word Music, 1986. Nondenominational, evangelical hymnal. Contemporary and traditional gospel songs, praise choruses, and traditional hymnody. Features a number of topical "brief services": responsive readings or Scriptures paired with two or more hymns relating to a theme. These lend themselves to devotional use.

The Hymnal of the Protestant Episcopal Church in the USA (1940). New York: The Church Pension Fund, 1940. Hymnody and service music in the Episcopal/Anglican tradition. A good resource if you would like to learn some Protestant chants. Offers "Principles of Chanting" as well as "Directions for Chanting."

The Illustrated Family Hymn Book, ed. Tony Jasper. New York: Seabury and G. Schirmer, 1980. A selection of classic and contemporary hymns, gospel songs, and folk hymns, accompanied by a brief history of each one. Beautifully illustrated with classical and contemporary art work. Some of the hymns use the traditional English tunes, since this book was designed and produced in Great Britain.

The Mennonite Hymnal. Newton, KS and Scottdale, PA: Herald, 1969. From the Anabaptist-Mennonite tradition. Wide selection of traditional hymns, German hymns (several in both German and English), and a section on "Peace and Nonresistance."

Service Book and Hymnal. Lutheran Church in America (now ELCA). Minneapolis: Augsburg; Philadelphia: Board of Publication, 1958. Traditional Lutheran hymnody, including chorales of both German and Swedish origin. Also includes liturgy, prayers, and service music.

The United Methodist Hymnal. Nashville: United Methodist Publishing House, 1989. Contains a wide variety of styles: traditional and contemporary hymns, ethnic hymns, gospel songs, spirituals, and praise choruses; a large selection of hymns and poems by Charles Wesley; and a liturgical Psalter with responses, some of which are simple phrases from familiar hymns.

Worship: A Hymnal and Service Book for Roman Catholics. Third Edition. Chicago: GIA Publications, 1986. Classic and contemporary hymns, chants, service music, and liturgy from the Roman Catholic tradition. The pew edition contains only melody line and lyrics. Parts and accompaniment sold separately.

The Worshiping Church: A Hymnal. Carol Stream, IL: Hope Publishing, 1990. Nondenominational hymnal. Offers a wide variety of traditional and contemporary hymns, gospel songs, spirituals, praise choruses, psalms and canticles, readings, and responses.

Songbooks

Glory and Praise. Phoenix: North American Liturgy Resources, 1984. Contemporary worship and praise music from the Roman Catholic tradition. Pew edition contains only melody line and lyrics. Accompaniment sold separately.

Maranatha! Music Praise & Worship Collection. Nashville: Maranatha! Music, Benson, 1987. Wide selection of contemporary praise choruses.

Music from Taizé. 2 vols. Chicago: GIA Publications, 1984. Responses, litanies, acclamations, and canons from the Taizé Community in France. Each volume is available in several different editions (people's, vocal, instrumental, etc.) and recordings.

The Other Songbook. Compiled by Dave Anderson. Phoenix: Fellowship Publications, 1984, 1987. Classic hymns, gospel favorites, children's songs, and praise choruses.

Songs of the Vineyard. (Several volumes.) Anaheim: Mercy, 1987–1994. A series of songbooks used by Vineyard Churches throughout the world. Many original songs emphasize intimacy and worship.

Songs of Zion. Nashville: Abingdon, 1981. Songbook in the African American tradition published by the United Methodist Church. Contains hymns, spirituals, black Gospel music, and service music. Includes performance suggestions and historical overview of music in the black worship experience.

Other Resources

Dallimore, Arnold A. *A Heart Set Free: The Life of Charles Wesley.* Westchester, IL: Crossway, 1988. Recent biography of Charles Wesley.

Havergal, Maria V. G. *Memorials of Frances Ridley Havergal.* New York: Anson D. F. Randolph, 1880. A biography of Frances Ridley Havergal, written by her sister. Out of print but worth a search.

Handbook to the Baptist Hymnal. Nashville: Convention Press, 1992. An inexpensive yet very good recent hymnal handbook. (Many handbooks run in the forty-dollar range. This one is in the twenty-dollar range.) Features the history of all the hymns and songs, authors and composers included in *The Baptist Hymnal.*

The Hymn Society in the United States and Canada. P.O. Box 30854, Fort Worth, TX 76129. Phone 800-THE-HYMN. Offers a quarterly publication regarding hymns and hymnology (*The Hymn: A Journal of Congregational Song*), an annual conference centering on hymns, and a book service featuring a wide and international selection of hymnals, songbooks, and hymn-related literature.

Osbeck, Kenneth W. *Amazing Grace: 366 Inspiring Hymn Stories for Daily Devotions.* Grand Rapids, MI: Kregal, 1990. Devotional book based upon traditional hymns and gospel songs, incorporating a brief history of each one.

RENOVARÉ Resources. A series of books designed for use by both individuals and groups and based upon the RENOVARÉ vision and practical strategy for spiritual growth. Published by HarperSanFrancisco. RENOVARÉ also offers a selection of devotional literature drawn from the five Christian traditions. RENOVARÉ, 8 Inverness Drive East, Suite 102, Englewood, CO 80112-5609. FAX: 303-792-0146.

Ruffin, Bernard. *Fanny Crosby.* Westwood, NY: Barbour, 1976. Biography of Fanny Crosby. Also gives insight into the development of the gospel hymn and the late nineteenth-century revival in America, including the work of D. L. Moody and Ira Sankey.

Ryden, E. E. *The Story of Christian Hymnody.* Rock Island, IL: Augustana, 1959. A history of Christian hymnody, presented in the context of the spiritual struggles and victories of the Church through the ages.

Schalk, Carl F. *Luther on Music: Paradigms of Praise.* St. Louis, MO: Concordia, 1988. A compilation and synopsis of Luther's writings regarding music.

Translations and Annotations of Choral Repertoire. Vol. 1. *Sacred Latin Texts.* Compiled and annotated by Ron Jeffers. Corvallis, OR: Earthsongs, 1988. Includes virtually every historical sacred Latin text you would hope to encounter, whether it be a liturgical one such as the *Gloria in Excelsis,* or a hymn such as the *Te Deum.* Gives the origin and liturgical context of each one, the Latin text with English inter-lined, a readable prose rendering, and a guide to pronunciation.

Walker, Wyatt Tee. *"Somebody's Calling My Name": Black Sacred Music and Social Change.* Valley Forge, PA: Judson, 1979. Traces the history of black sacred music and its relationship to social change.

Some of these books are out of print, but often they can be found in libraries, used bookstores, book sales, and garage sales. Churches that are getting new hymnals sometimes sell their old treasures at a low price. If you get the opportunity, you might consider purchasing four or five hymnals alike for family or small-group singing. In addition to the above sources, used and out-of-print Christian books are available by mail order from:

Book Search Service, 206 Pebble Lane, Clinton, MS 39056; 800-258-9802. Specializes in church music and hymnology, both new and used.

Eighth Day Books, 3700 E. Douglas #40, Wichita, KS 67208; 800-841-2541. Offers a catalog featuring classic works of Christian spirituality and devotional literature.

Kregel Publications, P.O. Box 2607, Grand Rapids, MI 49501-2607, 616-459-9444.

Index of Hymn Titles

Index of Authors and Composers